D1221511

Write for Recovery

Exercises for heart, mind and spirit

DIANE SHERRY CASE

Write for Recovery
Exercises for Heart, Mind and Spirit
All Rights Reserved.
Copyright © 2018 Diane Sherry Case
v1.0

The opinions expressed in this manuscript are solely the opinions of the author and do not represent the opinions or thoughts of the publisher. The author has represented and warranted full ownership and/or legal right to publish all the materials in this book.

This book may not be reproduced, transmitted, or stored in whole or in part by any means, including graphic, electronic, or mechanical without the express written consent of the publisher except in the case of brief quotations embodied in critical articles and reviews.

Miraculous Books Publishing

ISBN: 978-0-578-19435-6

Cover illustration by Lou Beach. Cover design by Ron Meckler. © 2018 All rights reserved - used with permission.

PRINTED IN THE UNITED STATES OF AMERICA

TABLE OF CONTENTS

I have forced myself to begin writing when I have been utterly exhausted, when I've felt my soul as thin as a playing card, when nothing has seemed worth enduring for another five minutes… and somehow the activity of writing changes everything.

— JOYCE CAROL OATES, *THE PARIS REVIEW INTERVIEWS, III*

FOREWORD

I have used writing as a form of therapy most of my life, journaling almost daily since I was ten and then writing fiction for twenty-five years. And while I've had many different kinds of traditional therapy, writing has been *at least* an equal source of healing, growth and change.

So I was not too surprised, when I began to teach incarcerated teens, at how quickly my students learned to love playing with words, even if it resulted in diving deep and telling very difficult stories. I saw their spirits lift as their creativity awakened. I later facilitated workshops with adults, and soon found myself doing workshops with psychotherapists. The results were so powerful and the exercises so effective that I was granted a license to teach therapists to use writing in their practices.

Write for Recovery is derived from the field of creative writing and uses the same type of exercises that are taught to inspire fiction writers. I combined my MFA in Creative Writing with my training as a psychotherapist and came up with fun ways to do some therapeutic work/play.

Among the many goals of these exercises is to help you explore the depths of both your positive and negative emotions, work with metaphors and imagery, create safe places within, cultivate mindfulness and define your most passionate goals. The wonderful side effect of this playful work is that free-flow writing awakens your creative spirit, allowing you to access the hidden talents that lie within you.

Writing is a door into your perceptions, emotions and thoughts, often revealing more to you than you consciously knew. It can serve to heal wounds, express hope and teach more about the self. It is an opportunity to see patterns and repetitions you wouldn't otherwise notice as striking. It helps you keep current in your emotions and explore your relationships to yourself, to other people and to the world. It can aid in the search for meaning and purpose in your life, helping you to let go of fear and begin to make steps toward your ultimate ideal life.

Last but not least, creative writing is simply uplifting! I believe that people are by nature creative beings. And believe it or not, literary talent is actually quite common. So if you do not think you have it in you – I plan to prove you wrong. I'm excited to share my joy of writing with you!

INTRODUCTION

Throughout the centuries, writers have explored their relationships to themselves, to other people and to the world, searching within to find life's purpose and meaning. Personal and intimate writing, usually in the form of diary or memoir, has been used at least since *The Confessions of St. Augustine* in the late 300s CE.

But it wasn't until the 1960s that the field of psychotherapy began to recognize writing as a healing modality. Dr. Ira Progoff, a depth psychologist who studied with Carl Jung, developed a method of structured journaling. In Progoff's words, he sought to "clarify personal relationships, address career concerns, face transitions, meet change, overcome blockages, deal with past hurts and present difficulties, gain new insights, and integrate life experiences."

Progoff's methods had only a brief period of popularity and, to the best of my knowledge no research has been done on the effectiveness of his workshops. And rather than build on or even continue Progoff's work, the field of psychology seemed to take a huge step back in the last few decades. Instead of structured exercises, people have simply been given the directive to journal about traumatic events. In nearly all the research done, the instructions to the participants have simply been to journal, the most commonly utilized method of therapeutic writing in the field today.

So although "journaling" has become very popular, more eclectic forms of therapeutic writing seem to have vanished from the field. The only other form of writing that is generally utilized is in the form of homework given by Cognitive Behavioral therapists, which consists of rewriting patterns of negative thinking. That is all fine and good, but it is a very left-brain process, the antithesis of an expressive art therapy.

James Pennebaker began to do research on the efficacy of therapeutic writing about twenty-five years ago and is considered the "grandfather" of the field. The research he did and all the studies since then regarding the effects of writing on both psychological and physical health has been very positive, indicating that indeed writing about both positive and negative events promotes both physical and psychological health. But the directive in nearly all of this research has simply been something to the effect of "write about a traumatic event." Expressive or therapeutic writing has basically regressed to simple journaling.

At least thirty studies on self-disclosure in the form of journal writing have shown that just twenty minutes a week of journaling improves health, both physical and psychological. But sometimes being told to just journal is not enough. The exercises in this book include both psychological and spiritual tools designed to lift one to a more positive level of well-being. You will go beyond the therapeutic journal, using creative writing exercises both in a playful spirit and as a method to delve deep into the psyche.

Some Psychological Theories Behind These Exercises

(If you prefer to skip to the exercises – just dive in!)

While I was studying for my Masters in Psychology, I discovered that I was intuitively using many psychological theories, such as classic Freudian psychoanalytic practices, which include free association. Free-association is considered the "fundamental rule" of psychoanalysis. The idea is to suspend self-censorship in order to unearth subconscious memories, feelings and desires. This is why I ask my students to write faster than they think, thereby bypassing the rational mind and surprising themselves with what they write.

Another one of my tools is to use paintings and photographs as inspiration for writing, in a similar way that tests, such as the Thematic Apperception Test and the Rorschach Test, have been used to diagnose patients. This method gives you a peek into your psyche, providing an opportunity to recognize stories and themes from your life. Alternatively, the same exercises can be used just for fun and fiction. Awakening your creative spirit, especially if it has been dormant for some time, is in itself quite liberating.

In Jungian therapy, dream analysis is sometimes used to gain insight into unresolved or buried feelings. When you are dreaming, your defenses are down, and you often have thoughts, feelings and images in your dreams that you would never be conscious of in day-to-day life. Once you start recording your dreams, you tend to remember subsequent dreams more often and more vividly.

One of the tenets of Carl Rogers' person-centered therapy is that therapists need to be more present and in the moment with their clients. In the same way, the discipline of mindfulness teaches you to be more present and in the moment with yourself, your environment and your relationships. Roger's teachings are about acceptance of where you are so that you are able to let go of your defenses and rigidity and perceive the world from different perspectives.

It was actually Carl Rogers' daughter, Natalie, who expanded some of his beliefs about human nature and creativity as she began to explore expressive arts therapies. She learned that through the arts, her clients gained more insight into both positive and negative emotions. But her work, for the most part, was centered around the visual arts and music.

Another idea that underlies expressive arts therapies is that working through challenging emotions expands resilience and aids in self-actualization. The value of these two goals in mental health is exhibited in the work of many theorists including, but not limited to, Carl Jung, Fritz Perls, Helen Bonny, and more recently Dan Siegel and Alan Schore.

Fritz Perls and Laura Perls stressed the importance of our relationship with both our environment and with other people. I often use dialogue with different parts of myself. You can do the same with yourself, with other people in your lives, as well as dialogues about both sides of a problem you might be facing. A few prompts involve describing the flavor and feelings of the places in which you live and work. One of my clients actually moved from one house to another after doing these exercises and realizing the negativity or lack of nourishment she was receiving from the environment in which she was living.

Gestalt Therapy, which was developed by Perls, has a component of mindfulness — being mindful of how you use your physical body. Another method I employ is written body scans and dialogues with different parts of one's body, hearing what those parts have to tell you.

Gestalt therapists are very interested in the language used by their clients, and a lot of the vocabulary they seek to change in their patients is part of the editing work I do, even aside from therapeutic writing. When working on a piece of fiction I edit out most qualifiers – "perhaps," "I guess," "sort of" – in favor of more direct language. Indirect language, such as "it is impossible for a sixty-year-old woman to find a man," gives the character no responsibility or ownership of the problem. Gestalt therapists prefer "I" statements, as in "I find it difficult to date."

Gestalt Therapy is also very much about the here and now in the therapy room, which is consistent with the idea of being mindful of our day-to-day activities. The age-old practice of mindfulness is quickly coming into the mainstream of psychotherapy because the results are so quickly evident. Mindfulness training, borrowed from Eastern philosophies, is also a big part of the relatively new Dialectical Behavioral Therapy, which teaches a combination of mindfulness training along with Cognitive Behavioral techniques.

Many of the exercises in the Write For Recovery program were created to cultivate a person's awareness of the ever present "Now." Exercises like simply writing down the sounds you hear, for example, or writing about washing the dishes in slow motion, savoring the warmth of the water on your hands, remind you to be aware of the present, rather than just rushing through the task while worrying about this and that, causing you to miss the experience of the moment.

Existential theory teaches you to utilize the knowledge that you are going to die in order to choose how you would like to live. Facing our mortality encourages us to value each moment as if it were our last.

Viktor Frankl's *Man's Search for Meaning* greatly influenced me. I try to use some of his ideas in my workshops, teaching people that although they may not have control over their circumstances, they always have the freedom to choose their attitude towards what life throws them. When you rewrite your story from that more creative point of view, you realize that you are not the victim of your fate.

As Irvin Yalom says in his book *Love's Executioner*: "Freedom is to be responsible for one's own choices, actions and one's own life situations." He goes on to quote Sartre who uses the words, "To be the author of," his or her own life design. Sartre's uncanny use of the word "author" could not be more relevant to a writing program.

Yalom opens his book by telling us that he often asks his patients the simple question, "What do you want?" He reports what I have experienced when I use this question in my workshops, that he has seen the question "evoke powerful unexpected emotions." I believe that writing the question, as opposed to *thinking* about it over and over allows the answers to come from a deeper place, and the "author" to go into more detail about what he or she does want, and what it would feel like to have this desire or longing met. The process definitely stays with you for days, as you evaluate and reevaluate the way you are responding to your own answers, offering you the opportunity to take responsibility for the choices you make.

It would seem logical, since Cognitive Behavioral Therapy is a lot about *rewriting* the negative messages you say to yourself, that I would have my students do a lot of work of that sort. But the very fact that it is a more logical process is precisely why I do so little of it. My preference is to stay away from the rational mind and trick the intellect to get out of our way, so that you can reach the creativity that lies deeper in your soul, and channel the wisdom that comes from somewhere beyond your mind.

LET'S DIVE IN!

Get ready to play with words and imagery, recover some long-lost memories, make friends of your enemies, talk to your ghosts, create soothing resources, peek inside your heart and rekindle lost dreams.

In the body of this book, I will share a few personal stories and some folk wisdom as I play around with metaphors from nature. Each topic could warrant a whole volume, but the prose is only a frame – a jumping-off point for the exercises. So I simply talk a little bit about my experiences and include a few words of wisdom, either earned or learned.

But you really don't have to even read it – you can just do the exercises if you like. Feel free to flip through and find whatever you are drawn to. Sometimes it is valuable to write about things you resist, but it is not necessary to go straight through the book from beginning to end. The only thing I will ask is that when you do a set of exercises, you do the whole set, in order. I begin each set with a warm-up, then delve into deeper issues and end the session with more uplifting exercises — inspirational prompts, prompts that will help you develop more mindfulness, create soothing imagery, or perhaps peer into your dreams and design plans to make them come true. So don't stop right after you do the more challenging exercises. My intention is that you end each session feeling lighter.

In the spirit of using intuition and following creative impulses, I have gone with my initial instinct to explore metaphors from the natural elements of water, fire, earth and air as well as the elements that make up our life – body, mind and spirit. I have organized the book using those headings, relating fire to rage, passion and creativity for example, or water to tears, thirst and "going with the flow." Sometimes it's a stretch, but humor me. I wouldn't be writing this if it weren't fun to write!

By the way, I am by no means claiming to be "recovered." I don't think there's such a thing. Recovery is a process and I certainly do not want to minimize any of the issues of recovery. Nor is this book meant to replace traditional psychotherapy. But it is a good adjunct to therapy as it sheds light on material you can bring to your therapist, thereby making more progress in a shorter amount of time.

There seems to be no finish line to recovery, and everybody is either doing it or going downhill. I believe that the trauma I have bounced back from, the grief I learned from and the resilience that has kept me alive, left me with a few tools and ways of perceiving the world that may help you. I am frankly amazed that I am still standing, much less thriving, vital, prolific and happy as I enter the seventh decade of my life. But loss is inevitable, and you never know what will happen next. Life seems to be a series of things to recover from and many of them, like the death of a loved one or a serious addiction, may be issues you will need to revisit throughout your life. Even if you shut the door on them, they still become part of who you are, who you have become. And if you carry them with awareness, the empathy you develop becomes a gift that will connect you more deeply to friends and family. Your resilience becomes an inspiration.

As I've said, most of these prompts are designed to bypass the intellect and get straight to the unconscious and/or the emotions. When you tap into those sources, you are often gifted with a feeling like "channeling," when words just pour effortlessly onto the page. As an actor and a writer, I learned to experience that state of being in which I relinquished my goals, judgment, even my fear of looking foolish. It is from that place that the work begins to feel like it is coming effortlessly through you, not from you. The main reason I love to write is because in the process, I learn things about myself, and the world, that I didn't previously know. My writing is, at best, wiser than I am. So these ideas are not something I use solely as a therapeutic tool – they are also the basis of my work as an artist.

You will also begin to notice themes that run through your life. When writing fiction, I am often surprised by what I wrote. I find themes are woven throughout the novel or short story with no conscious planning on my part. So you may discover things in what you've written that you had no idea you knew.

One method I'll use to help you get out of your own way is to give you simple prompts like lists, or a few keywords. Another way to free your mind is to use art to inspire you. A favorite song, perhaps the one you love to cry to, a photograph of a place that looks familiar, a painting of a woman who has something to tell you. So begin to gather some art books or photographs that you are drawn to, as we will refer to them later.

I always suggest writing fast, before you have time to think. You do not need to form sentences or pay attention to spelling or punctuation. Feel free to veer off into whatever words flow in the moment, following that vein, and returning to the exercises when you are ready. If you get stuck, write about writing, write about being stuck. As long as you keep the pen moving, you're doing just fine.

Please set aside any expectations of your writing. Let go of critical thoughts and judgments. Keep in mind that you are not writing for anyone but yourself, even though you may choose to share it with others. If you haven't written much before, you may find hidden talents. But please don't try to write well. If that happens — what a pleasant surprise, but it is not what this is about. And while seasoned writers will definitely come up with a wealth of material for your next novel, poem, song, memoir or even script, please don't make that your goal.

Write your exercises and journal entries as if you were going to burn them. Put out the welcome mat for surprises. Let go of the tendency to want things to be this way or that. There is no right way or wrong way to do these exercises. Some are creative writing exercises, adapted or designed in a way that promotes growth and healing. Others are simply questions – not to ponder – but to write about in an improvisational way. You may wish to close your eyes or take some breaths for a few moments now and then, but only to get in touch with feelings or see images, not to think about what you are going to say.

I suggest writing by hand on good-sized paper, not a tiny notebook. (It doesn't give you room to flow write.) If you are more comfortable with a computer, that's fine too. But there is something about writing longhand that seems to get you slightly closer to intuitive, instinctual writing.

This program is designed to create changes in your day-to-day life. Whether I use psychological techniques to assist you in changing negative thinking patterns or assignments that help cultivate mindfulness and other spiritual principles, my hope is that you will not only do the exercises, you will use them to transform your life. The life you craft is, after all the most important piece of art you will ever create!

NOTE: Though writing about painful things is often healing, the most important thing is for you to feel safe. If any of these exercises feel threatening to you, by all means skip them, or at least tread lightly. Instead, do one of the more "now" or "future" oriented writing assignments. I have tried to find a good balance between exploration and healing, between exercises that are revealing about the past and ones that give you ideas and tools to help you navigate the present and future.

WARM UP

Take five deep breaths. Breathe in to the count of four, hold four, breathe out four, hold four, etc.

Then take note of your five senses – in the here and now. See what's around you – note the colors and textures. Feel what is supporting your body, the fabric and the air on your skin, as well as anything else that stands out. Listen to the sounds around you. Become aware of any smells or tastes. Be present!

These two warm ups are always good preparation for a writing session. Now you are in the moment and ready to go!

EXERCISES

A) This is a free-association exercise called "I Remember." Below is a list and I invite you to write brief sentences or phrases in response to each of the items below. If one item doesn't resonate for you, just skip it and go on to the next. Each sentence or phrase will begin with "I remember..."

I REMEMBER...

An object in the house of your grandmother or other older relative

A person who you wish you could see again

A day you'll never forget

A time when you felt strong and powerful

Traveling somewhere you'd never been

A photograph etched in your mind

A time when it was snowing

A particular holiday meal

A talisman or piece of jewelry

A piece of clothing

An object you've treasured

A phone call

A kiss

A car

A dream

An animal

A surprise

B) Now take one of those items,and expand on
it. That item at your grandma's house, for example,
where does that memory lead you? Try and fill a page.

C) Write a couple of sentences about your experience
doing this exercise. Were you surprised by any
memories you had not visited in a while? Did feelings
come up with any of the memories? Did you have
trouble because you do not remember a lot? (I have
blocked out years of my life because of trauma.)
Was the exercise pleasant and fun or was it perhaps
uncomfortable? It's different for everyone, and if this
exercise didn't light your fire, then read on!

It's the fire in my eyes,
And the flash of my teeth,
The swing in my waist,
And the joy in my feet.
— Maya Angelou

Watching the flickering shadows from my sandalwood scented candle, I am delightfully soothed. The way it always changes, this magical dancing art, created by a tiny colorful fire just doing its energetic thing.

Like water, fire is a shape-shifter. Candles, campfire, sunshine, hearth fire, wild fire. It can be warm and comforting as well as raging and destructive. Walking in the sunshine, I bask in the energy that fuels all living things. In front of the fireplace in winter, I am warm and meditative. The fires raging in Malibu remind me to contain my own flare-ups, to use that fiery energy for creativity and not destruction.

I see inner light in various forms – the warm place in your heart when you actually embrace an evening alone, the playful flicker of a flirtation or inspiration, the burning rage you hope to free yourself from and the fierce power that emerges from within when you need to fight for your life.

Life is full of unexpected sparks and leaps, waters thrown on warm hearth fires and flames that feel as if they may burn down the house. But there is also the sparkle in your eyes and the passions of a lifetime that long to be expressed. Think of your light as passion, creativity, playfulness and warmth. Those qualities are your life force.

WARM UP

Light My Fire, I'm on Fire, Ring of Fire. A lot of songwriters have used the metaphor of fire. Write your own song or poem (a poem can just be a list of phrases) using one of these titles.

EXERCISES

A) Complete these sentences:

I am curious about…

I secretly wish…

I would be truly happy if…

When I was younger I dreamed of…

I've always wished I could…

Even though it sounds silly, I would really like to…

If it were possible, I would…

Before I die, I want to…

B) What would your passion or passions be if you dared to think anything is possible? Describe what you can do to feed or realize that passion.

C) Draw a picture of two people and a fire (doesn't matter if you can't draw – stick figures are okay – colored ones are better.) The fire can be a campfire, a forest fire, a candle, lightning, any form of fire you can think of. Next, write a description of your drawing. Then tell what happened before the scene in the drawing, and what will happen afterwards. Voila, a little story!

Creativity – Letting Your Light Shine!

> If you don't use your creativity, it will use
> you!
> — UNKNOWN SOURCE

Years ago, when I went to Bali, I learned that there is not even a separate word for art in the Balinese language – it is the same as the word for human! In Bali, art is a natural way of life — every Balinese, no matter what their occupation, makes art whether it be music, dancing, puppets or flower arrangements. Making art is simply part of their culture and their religion, like a devotional practice.

I firmly believe that everyone is creative. Some people simply have not developed that part of themselves. One of my favorite things about facilitating workshops is watching my clients delight when they have written something they like. Literary talent is actually quite common, as I am sure most talents are. It is just a matter of spending time and energy both being playful and learning a craft. And the rewards are endless. They include the uplifting feeling of delight, a leap out of the ordinary and a healthy outlet for all sorts of feelings.

Creativity has always been my saving grace, and when I neglect that part of myself, I am (frankly) screwed. I get cranky, depressed, I don't feel centered — something is off. I might start obsessing on some insignificant event or wallow in regret or imagine the worst of all possible outcomes for every aspect of my life. I might become a hypochondriac, convincing myself that the bugbite on my body is a lump of cancer or the headache is a brain tumor. It deserves repeating: If you don't use your imagination, it will use you!

Thank God, I have finally learned to identify the symptoms of creative starvation, even the early signs, like feeling "off-center," and I don't let it get that far. Once I even had the common sense to do a huge project right after a breakup with a lover, and it sure did help me get over it quickly.

But during my divorce from the father of my kids, I let myself stagnate creatively and lost years of vital productivity. I had just finished directing my second short film when my ex-husband and I broke up and perhaps the history of my mother undermining my artistic endeavors, coupled with the fact that he left while I was directing, made me gun shy. I must have reverted into fear of repercussions for "letting my little light shine."

In any event, for whatever reason, I simply forgot that I needed to make art to survive. I stopped directing, I stopped writing, I wasn't acting, I didn't even go to the film festivals in which my film was an official selection. I do not believe I've ever gone that long without expressing myself artistically and I sure suffered the consequences. My grief and anger were so large that I abandoned myself. Feelings ran rampant with no outlet. And my imagination used me to no end! I had all of the fantasies scorned lovers dwell on, like dropping him off by helicopter into the Alaskan wilderness--stark naked. My wicked daydreams let a little liveliness bubble up, but they didn't take the place of actually creating. I considered writing a book on humorous and harmless jokes to play on your ex-husband, like putting a pair of his favorite black lace thongs in the suit jacket he had left behind, so he can accidently pull them out while he's at dinner with his new woman. Frivolous, but at least it would have been some form of expression. But instead of writing, I just smothered my rage and trudged an uphill battle — survival without joy.

Those years after my divorce (and the sudden death of my only sibling, which happened around the same time) would have been so much easier and I would have healed much more quickly if I had kept on writing, or even taken up painting or photography, dancing or singing. Anything to give the flames some air instead of throwing blankets over them. The blankets didn't put the fires out — they just caused a lot of filthy black smoke that made it hard to breathe.

I sure learned my lesson. Being creative is not a luxury--it is a ne-
cessity. Especially when the shit hits the fan and you feel paralyzed.
That is when it is most critical to make a little effort toward doing
something that feeds your soul. Even ten minutes a day of writing
or making a collage or singing to yourself will uplift you, make you
stronger, help you find meaning in the mess.

When I am creating I feel liberated, centered, focused and whole.
I see hope, dreams and possibilities, even meaning, often bigger than
my own little world. Once in a while, I will read something I've written and say to myself, "Wow! Now that makes sense. Who knew?"

If you have not integrated some form of art into your life, there
is no better time to do it than now. I am so glad you are writing and
hope you commend yourself for giving yourself this gift. I hand out
playful stickers to my students to put on their calendars for each day
they allocate at least ten minutes to their art of choice.

If you already have a vital creative life, make sure you touch base
with it every single day, even if it is just for a few minutes. If you let
a project lie dormant it soon becomes overwhelmingly difficult to
come back to. So "touch" your art each day, even if it is brief. The
other benefit of this is that your subconscious will be working on
it between sessions, and as you may recall my saying, your subconscious is a lot more imaginative than you are!

WARM UP

Breathe and check in with your senses.

List the art forms to which you are attracted. Plan a date to explore one of them.

EXERCISES

A) Close your eyes and imagine that you are at the threshold of a doorway. You open it and find a fireplace or candles burning brightly. You will also see a person or maybe two. After you've spent some time imagining the scene, describe everything you see, smell, feel and hear. What color are the walls? What does it smell like? Is the person moving?

B) Find a painting or photo that you are attracted to, one that has at least one person in it. Describe the painting. Then write a story telling what is happening in the painting, what happened before and what will happen after. Make sure you use all of your senses – imbue the subject of the artwork with smells, textures, sounds, etc.

When you are finished, read it aloud to yourself. If something relates to you or you find metaphors, notice and reflect on them. If the exercise was simply pleasant, note that a vacation from your rational mind and some delight in your creativity goes a long way!

RAGE

> If we could read the secret history of our
> enemies, we should find in each man's life
> sorrow and suffering enough to disarm all
> hostility.
>
> — HENRY WADSWORTH LONGFELLOW

In his book entitled *Anger*, Thich Nhat Hanh talks about running after the arsonist when your house is on fire. Better to put out the fire first. He suggests that instead of reacting automatically when someone acts in a way that is hurting you, practice mindful breathing.

If you nurse your anger and hold on to it, you develop the toxic energy of resentment. Resentments can be monumental or small, usually when someone gets in the way of what you want or how you think things should be. Consider that they may be doing you a favor. Who are you to say how things should be?

Anger can sometimes be constructive and protect you in a healthy way, so it is important to listen to what your anger is trying to tell you. You may need to straighten out a situation in your life, change or even leave a job or relationship.

Anger becomes destructive when you turn it in on yourself and end up depressed or even in bed, suffocating in your own smoke. And of course you don't want to let it burn rampant, destroying all in its path, burning down the metaphoric home you are living in. Better to simply confront your anger with curiosity. It turns out that venting too much, even getting it out on paper too many times, can sometimes fuel the fire. Trauma and rage are both emotions that can be fueled by overfocusing on them. So just write about it once and do it with curiosity, asking yourself questions about your anger. Is there another emotion hiding behind it? Lack of control, sadness, fear, frustration…

When I was in my early twenties, I was self-destructive with drugs and alcohol. Anger had been taboo in my family of origin, especially for children, and with all that bottled-up rage I became an angry young woman. Unfortunately, I abused myself instead of expressing it.

What saved my life was acting class. I was able to channel that anger into creativity. It was like taking my soul out of a deep dark dungeon and letting it loose onstage, expressing dynamic person-alities that up until then had never existed. I created entire people, giving my body a brand new brightly burning heart.

Perhaps the most important tool for letting go of anger is for-giveness. I have written about forgiving in the section entitled SOUL. Forgiving is not only spiritual, it is quite practical. I just heard a great saying about holding on to resentments – it is like taking a poison pill and expecting the other to die. In other words, you are the one who will suffer.

So let it out and then let it go--see what you learned and give yourself a nod for wisely moving forward with a little more peace of mind.

WARM UP

I won't say it anymore but start each session with breath work and checking in with your senses.

Write a fantasy revenge –a comedy – a humorous way you might imagine getting even.

(Don't get too ugly, please.)

EXERCISES

A) So who are you angry at? Where does it hurt? Track it in your body. Then write a letter to that person. Say anything you like – express your feelings wholeheartedly – for afterwards you are going to take the letter and burn it!

B) How do you express your anger? What would be a more skillful, healthier way? And how would you feel without your anger? Lighter? Empty? Is your anger serving any purpose? How could that purpose be better served?

C) Write about a situation you are angry at from the other person's point of view.

Hearth Fire — Warmth

My heart is delighting in an atmosphere of warmth, as I just had a holiday party; and I can still feel spirits of many people I love, respect and appreciate, all gathered together in my home. I don't ever invite anyone for any reason other than the fact I feel drawn to them, I feel a kinship, sincerity or warmth. I don't have people in my life for ulterior motives. Surely I would have been more successful if I could have tolerated such relationships, but it is just not my nature, nor is it how I want to spend my time. And the reward is that it feels like the wood in my den is infused with good energy from the friends who visited my home.

There's a deep responsibility in having people in your life. Your friends may need people who help to keep their inner light glowing when the going gets tough. We all need to be there when others depend on us. And we also need to feel needed. In fact, one of the best ways to get close to someone is to reach out for help. Most people I am drawn to welcome the opportunity to give emotional or even physical support, whenever I dare to ask. So don't hesitate to reach out and give someone the opportunity to help you!

WARM UP

Write about a time you helped someone.

Write about a time someone helped you.

EXERCISES

A) What brings you warmth? Who or what helps you feel cozy? How can you bring more warmth into your home?

B) Find a painting or photo of a fire. (You can just do an online search.) Write about the image using all five senses.

C) Next, write a paragraph, poem or little story using the fire in the image as a metaphor.

D) Have dinner (or a bath) by candlelight!

> I draw sweet air
> Deeply and long,
> As pure as prayer,
> As sweet as song.
> — ROBERT WILLIAM SERVICE

We start breathing as soon as we come out of the womb and we don't stop until we die. Isn't it incredible how little appreciation we have for the air that sustains us — how we take it for granted? How about giving it some respect!

I once called my friend, Ann, when I was full of anxiety and fear. I wanted her to listen to my sad story and tell me how to feel good. All she said was, "Go outside, take a deep breath, and look at the sky."

I followed directions for once. I opened my back door, went outside and looked up at the sky. I instantly felt better, my problems humbled by the expanse of space above me, my soul soothed by the wonder of the sky. My body relaxed with each exhale.

One of the most valuable mindfulness tools I gave my children was to constantly remind them to breathe, especially when they were stressed or upset. I have found that a few deep breaths will help any kind of discomfort, pain or anxiety.

Probably as a result of trauma in my early life, I often notice that I have just plain forgotten to breathe. I think many of us do this when we are stressed, though we usually aren't even aware of it. Begin to notice how many times in the day you catch yourself simply not breathing, not inviting life in nor letting energy out. Perhaps, as I have done, you repress feelings by holding your breath.

A long-ago lover taught me a way to fall asleep that I have never forgotten. When in bed with another, synchronize your breath with theirs. It always brings a calm that leads to sleep. I am not sure if that is because of the limbic attunement that it creates, or because it is a form of meditation.

Breath is the most important element in a yoga practice, a way

of bringing life force into your body, and staying in the present moment. It is the breath that bridges the mind and body.

I generally start my workshops by asking people to take a few
deep breaths and settle in. I have suggested using that as a ritual
whenever you sit down to write.

WARM UP

Be conscious of your breath for five full minutes. Your
mind will wander, but keep bringing it back to the
breath. Focus on wherever you feel it in your body
— your stomach, chest, throat or nose. Try counting
breaths to stay connected. There is no success or
failure at this!

EXERCISES

A) Next, write about what that mini-meditation was
like. Where did your mind go? Did you ever catch
yourself simply not breathing? What is the quality of
your breath — deep, shallow, slow?

B) Go outside and look up at the sky. Write about
how it makes you feel.

C) Write about the name you were given at birth. Is
there a story behind it?

Rainbow Of Emotions

> Whatever you do, don't try and escape from
> your pain, but be with it. Because the attempt
> to escape from pain creates more pain.
> — TIBETAN BOOK OF LIVING AND DYING

"You're just too sensitive" is a phrase my dad used to reprimand me with. And as a younger woman, I was often so overwhelmed by my emotions that I feared I wouldn't survive them. I tried to get rid of them, disown them, kill the nasty pests. I attempted to hide my emotions from others as well as myself.

The most valuable advice I have found on dealing with emotions is to observe them with curiosity. Most of us look at negative emotions with aversion, and if you've been traumatized, you may have learned to disassociate, more or less "leaving your body" when strong feelings surface. I still catch myself being rather flippant when I am uncomfortable with my feelings.

Sometimes you may stuff your emotions so deeply that you can't even find them. You may misplace your anger at work onto others (as when someone is angry at his boss and instead kicks his dog.) You might even "somatize" your emotions, a phenomenon in which the body knows what you do not consciously feel, causing such things as headaches or stomachaches.

Or you may have the unfortunate skill of escaping the present moment and abandoning yourself by keeping constantly busy, using drugs, eating, doing anything to run away from that which you do not want to feel. It is like you have left your body, checked out. This may stem from early childhood: an infant who did not get his or her needs met and learned to shut down and deny a painful situation he or she had no means to control. The question is, how do you live with those feelings today? How do you learn not to flee?

As I've mentioned, in my family of origin, anger was simply not okay. But my very first acting job, when I was ten years old, was a segment in a television show that was entitled "The Brat." In the show, the other actors wore shin pads and I got to kick them! I fell in love with acting immediately. I was very lucky to find out when I was young that expressing my anger through art was the safest, most constructive way to go. Often, when I write, I go deeper and find out what is really going on behind my defenses. Writing helps you to sink into your body, release feelings and uncover hidden thoughts so that you can sit peacefully with them instead of acting out unconsciously. It also helps to ground you in the present moment. Mindfulness, psychotherapy and creativity all bring you to a more conscious awareness of your emotions, and help you learn to simply allow those feelings to pass.

Another trap some people fall into is to try and tame or bury their emotions using rationality. It is considered an admirable trait, as in "rising above" feelings. But artists can't afford to do that, even if they are capable of it. Emotions are the tools of the trade, the source of inspiration. Inspiration (the root of which is "in spirit") is outside the range of rational thinking, as is love. To rise above or bury your emotions is to dampen your spirit, the vital force that puts the "live" in alive. Who wants to "rise above" love?

You can only feel positive emotions at the same depth that you allow yourself to feel negative emotions. Tuning out simply does not work. The emotions you are unaware of, the emotions that you avoid, affect your life whether you recognize it or not. They have got to come out in some form.

I have spent a lifetime searching for a way to live in peace with my emotions. Art has always been the answer for me. I now know that my sensitivity is a real blessing and that, artist or not, the expression of a broad range of normal emotions is essential if you want to fully live life.

WARM UP

Finish these sentences. Note your visceral response to each word.

I get angry when...

I am afraid that...

What gives me joy is...

I was surprised by...

What disgusts me is...

I am fearful when...

I experience shame when...

I feel envious about...

I feel judged if...

I get discouraged when...

I was hurt that...

I worry about...

I felt guilty about the time...

I feel hopeful when...

EXERCISES

A) Now go through the list again, and write about how each of these emotions was dealt with in your family of origin.

B) Rewrite the story of the emotions that trouble you in your life. For example: How would you like to deal with anger differently than it was dealt with in your family, or differently than you now handle it?

C) Write a dialogue between two opposing emotions, embodied as animals. Have fun with it!

Atmosphere

We are obviously blessed to all live together in an atmosphere that promotes life. Trees reach for the sky, birds migrate for miles and we all exist in life-giving oxygen.

But what about the smaller, more personal atmospheres you live with? Do they create space and encourage growth and expansion? Or are you, at times, living or working in a constricting atmosphere? Does your living space make you happy to be home?

I try to hang art on my walls that calms me in my bedroom, inspires me in my office and uplifts me in the living room. It is inexpensive to create nice lighting, perhaps even a colored light bulb, or a small mood lamp for before bedtime. The music you listen to also greatly affects the atmosphere of your home, as does the smell of fragrant candles.

Another major element of the atmosphere in which you live is the atmosphere you carry with you. Does it protect you, while still being permeable enough to let in the positive? Is the energy you create for yourself life-affirming? Infused with optimism? Are you looking for the goodness in every shattered soul you meet? Do you carry a sense of gratitude for the blessings in your life? Are you playful? Can you laugh at yourself and our common predicaments?

Envisioning a positive aura around you radiates outwards, sometimes in the form of charisma, attracting others to you. It can also be a protective space surrounding you, neutralizing toxins that invade your personal environment. The atmosphere you carry colors your perceptions of yourself as well as others. I actually love those old hippie exercises of imagining yourself with auras of different colors. You can change your mood if you change the energy that you emit.

When you become aware of the atmospheres you live in and realize that they are partly of your own creation, you will have more control over how you feel and a lot more light to give to others.

WARM UP

Write about the atmosphere you live in, your home or your work. Describe the feeling it instills: what is its weight, its color and density?

What would you like your environment to feel like — your ideal atmosphere? List things you can do to make your space more peaceful, inspiring and comfortable.

EXERCISES

A) Now describe the atmosphere that you carry with you — your aura, for lack of a better word. Is it sunny or dark? Heavy or light? What color? And what does the atmosphere that surrounds you communicate to others? Does it change from day to day?

B) Describe the ideal atmosphere you would like to carry with you. Then start practicing!

Silence

Give me silence and I will outdare the night.
— KAHLIL KIBRAN, *SAND AND FOAM*

We are all so inundated with noise, from the music at the supermarket to the constant input of our phones, televisions and traffic. Some of the noise in our lives is unavoidable, but much of it is self-inflicted out of a fear of silence. But our soul needs silence to be heard. Listening deeply adds a rich dimension to our lives.

The way you perceive silence and act in your silence defines you as much, if not more than, your words. If you are afraid of silence, you might talk a lot, text a lot, hang out on Facebook or have the television on all the time. But if you are at peace with yourself, you might revel in silence.

Sometimes I experience silence as boredom, or being alone as loneliness. But silence is ideally about allowing a soothing space for myself amidst the constant chatter and business of daily life. Think of rest, calm, peace. My wise friend, Ann, calls it "the pause that refreshes."

Time spent alone in silence is an opportunity for a more contemplative life, to develop a better relationship with yourself, to go deeper into your soul, and learn to make peace with solitude.

WARM UP

For five minutes write down every sound you hear, from your heartbeat to the sounds in the distance. Listen to the distance as if staring at the horizon.

EXERCISES

A) Discuss the dark side of silence in your life. Are you afraid to sit silently alone? Do silences in conversations make you uncomfortable?

B) Remember a time when silence felt like peace. It does not have to be a pure silence. For me, it was one night on my grandmother's farm, on the darkest of nights, when all I could hear was a symphony of insects. Describe the scene and then describe the feelings evoked.

Silence As Communication

> "Under all speech that is good for anything
> there lies a silence that is better. Silence is
> deep as Eternity; speech is shallow as Time."
> —THOMAS CARLYLE

Silence as communication is a fascinating phenomena. Think of the angry silences you have experienced, or the joyful silent sharing of a smile.

As an actor, I became very aware of subtext, the silent meaning of the spoken word. On stage, there is nothing more dreaded than an empty silence, for in life our silences are rarely empty. They can be full of fear or dread, joy or hope, love or hatred. But rarely full of nothing. You communicate more by what you do not say than what you do. Silence between two people can be a warm peace or it can be a venomous punishment.

People are often afraid of silence in conversation, but permitting that silence allows people to communicate from a deeper place. When you stop thinking of what you want to say next and let others know that you are really listening, even to the silences between their thoughts, you have a more respectful and soulful communication. I was once told "If God wanted you to talk more than you listened, he would have given you two mouths and one ear."

Some cultures enjoy company by just sitting with another, not suffering the urgency to fill the peaceful silence with chatter, just sharing solitude and the comfort of another's presence.

WARM UP

Find a painting with two people in it. Write what is said in the silences between them. Write what they are feeling, perhaps what they may want to say but don't.

EXERCISES

A) Do silences in conversations make you uncomfortable? Are you quick to fill them with chatter?

B) Are you aware of your nonverbal communications? Do you use silence as a weapon?

C) What would a pleasant night alone with yourself in silence look like? Describe the atmosphere you might create and what you would do with that precious time. Then – try it!

D) Write a dialogue (in paragraph form) between two people. The tricky part is that I am going to ask you not to use words. It is a silent dialogue. Write the subtext beneath the silence.

Music

Throughout history, music and dance have been associated with the spiritual. Music is almost always used in religious ceremonies, from trance-inducing drumming to Gregorian chants.

In his book *Awakenings*, Oliver Sacks talks about how people who have neurological problems and who often cannot move or talk can sometimes respond to music and even sing. People with Alzheimer's can often remember lyrics of songs they learned years ago, though the rest of their memory is gone.

Rhythmic music has been shown to actually create changes in brain waves. "We may be sitting on one of the most widely available and cost effective therapeutic modalities that ever existed.... Listening to music seems to be able to change brain functioning to the same extent as medication, in many circumstances," said Gabe Turow, a visiting scholar in the Department of Music at Stanford, where he organized a symposium that looked at therapeutic benefits of musical rhythm. They found that slow beats create a calm, meditative state, while faster beats may stimulate the brain to more alert states.

Music can also hold and awaken memories. My kids' father is a musician and for years after our divorce, I could not listen to his music. Then I realized that wonderful memories in my life are stored in those songs, and I reclaimed the good feelings of the memories by listening once again to the soundtrack of that period of my life.

There are songs that put me in a good mood and songs that make me cry. Sometimes I want a good cry and sometimes I want something to inspire me to wash the dishes!

WARM UP

What kind of music do you listen to now, and how does it make you feel?

EXERCISES

A) Chronicle the soundtrack of your life – listing all the songs you remember loving from childhood to the present.

B) Choose two or more of the songs, one sad and one happy, and write about the memories they bring up.

C) Make a playlist that is solely designed to uplift you.

The Winds Of Change

The pessimist complains about the wind;
The optimist expects it to change;
The realist adjusts the sails.
— WILLIAM ARTHUR WARD

One thing you can always count on is change. Hour by hour and day by day.

No matter how good or bad life's circumstances are for you, no matter how depressed or elated you are – this too shall pass. Success may be followed by grief and happiness may crash into disaster. The Buddha said that life is made of suffering, sickness, old age and death, and that once you realize that, you can relax and enjoy the moment. It sounds grim, but it is true.

The best you can do is stay open and not try to fight the inevitable. Why paddle a canoe when you can open your sails and glide with the wind?

And whether your fate for the present time is good fortune or bad news, there is no point in asking, "Why me?" The answer to that question is always, "Why not you?"

The word flight also brings to mind those especially high moments, when it feels like you are soaring through life and all is going well. We sometimes have just as hard a time with good times as bad. When all is going smoothly and you are gliding through life, it might feel unfamiliar or unsafe. You may even want to sabotage yourself.

Trust is your parachute. Trust that you are lovable and deserve good feelings. Trust that it is okay to have an easy ride once in a while. Soon you will be able to negotiate a soft landing. Just as it takes practice to endure hard times, sometimes it takes practice to enjoy life!

WARM UP

Write from the point of view of a bird, describing what it feels like to fly. Write it as if you yourself are flying, focusing on both the physical sensations and the emotions, which might run anywhere from fear to great freedom and joy. When you tire of flying, land softly in exactly the place you would most like to be. Describe it. Enjoy it!

EXERCISES

A) Make a list of the difficult changes that you have already survived.

B) What changes might you fear to go through in the future? What will make these changes bearable for you? What makes for a soft landing?

C) What is the most positive change you could make in your life right now? Write down the steps toward making this change.

> "We sink our roots deep into the black
> soil and draw power and being up into
> ourselves.... We feel grounded, centered, in
> touch with the ancient and eternal rhythms
> of life."
> — DAVID N. ELKINS, *HUMANISTIC PSYCHOLOGY, A
> CLINICAL MANIFESTO*

In most cultures Earth is considered a female deity. There are reasons why they call her Mother Earth. In her rich soil are all the nutrients needed for plant life. Literally tons of animals can survive on just an acre of land. Earth nurtures and nourishes us. And she's our only home.

Recently there has been some attention to the idea of "earthing," which is basically walking barefoot. The idea behind earthing is that our ancestors went barefoot, slept on the ground and were more connected to the earth's electromagnetic waves than we are. I do know that amongst my fondest memories are both running barefoot on my grandmother's farm and walking shoeless in the sand on many a beach. Both seem incredibly healing to me and now I enjoy an occasional barefoot stroll on my front lawn. The joy it brings reminds me of the joy I feel when looking up at the sky.

When you let yourself feel held by Mother Earth and open your eyes to her miracles, there is always a seed of hope, no matter how deep your grief or your wounds. Even when your soul feels like a desert, if you open your eyes, you will see at least a tiny bit of life.

After my only sister died suddenly at the age of thirty-four, I was in the darkest place I've ever known. The very first inkling of light, the first time I knew I could possibly survive the loss, was when I noticed that the peach tree in front of my house was bearing new fruit. I was surprised that I could feel even a moment of joy. It was a small but stunning vision of life.

WARM UP

Let's just do one fun prompt that I heard about from
my mentor, Jim Krusoe:

Write about a person alone in a room with a plant.
Make sure to use all of your senses – not just
the colors of sight, but sound, smell, taste, touch,
movement.

EXERCISES

A) Now look for the metaphors in what you wrote.
Notice if there's a theme that relates to your life.

B) Take your notebook for a walk. Get as close to
nature as you can. Write about a plant or a cloud or
an animal or all three, using each of your senses.

Rocks

I've already mentioned that I have been in therapy half of my life and still wouldn't call myself "recovered." In some areas of my life, I still struggle with the same damn issues. In his book *We've Had a Hundred Years of Psychotherapy*, Joseph Hillman looks at those things that won't be changed and won't go away as "Ore, rocks, that make for character, for the peculiar idiosyncrasy that you are....It's peculiar in our culture to believe that these things get ironed out."

I have come to realize that my original goals in therapy and writing were simply not realistic. I was looking to be healed, to be permanently comfortable, to rid myself of all the goodies that come with growing up in a dysfunctional family and having a lifetime full of traumas, big and small. I wanted all that history erased. I wanted to be perfectly happy all the time. That's what I imagined a "normal" healthy person would look like.

"Normal" people are quite rare, if they exist at all. So does that mean all the therapy and writing I did was in vain? No way! I feel generally content now, even with the ups and downs inherent in life, and I'm sure that if I had not taken care of myself, I would be a lot worse off. Expecting perfection is to fall victim to what Michael Ventura called "the basic premise of American life, which has infected therapy, namely, 'everything is supposed to be all right.'" Well, sometimes things simply aren't all right. You can't always resolve the problems of life. But you can become more conscious, and alter the course of your perceptions.

So my goal is no longer to be "cured." I have generally ceased judging myself as damaged goods. I no longer look at my shortcomings as ugly. I have stopped disowning my deep sadness. I have gotten to know that my wounds and scars are rich soil for creativity.

Perhaps, ultimately, recovery is simply a matter of awareness and acceptance — a sense of being grounded in truth. So forget being "fixed" or perfect or recovered. Make it your goal to strive toward recovery and realize there is no endgame. Even the Dalai Lama still meditates!

Awareness of your wounds also carries with it the profound gift of empathy. A gift that insists you listen, feel and understand in a way that lightens the load of others who may be suffering.

Scientific research explains why it feels good to help others. When you help someone, you actually create more of the neurotransmitter and hormone dopamine than the person on the receiving end. So giving is the name of the game.

WARM UP

List your goals in terms of healing. Then ask yourself
what your life would look like if these goals were met.

EXERCISES

A) With as much curiosity as you can, write about
your "treasured wound." That wound you have gotten
so used to, it seems like a precious part of you. What
is the price of carrying it? What do you get out of it?
What is beneath it? Do you still need it? What would
it feel like to let it go?

B) In the form of a letter, tell yourself that you will
love and accept the part of you that may feel damaged.
Affirm that you are lovable in spite of, or along with,
all of your character defects. You can make the letter
from yourself to yourself or you can make it from
God to you or from a person who loves you.

Animal Instincts

"When we walk mindfully and touch the
Earth with our feet...we get healed."
—THICH NHAT HANH, *TOUCHING PEACE*

"Creation gave us instincts for a purpose. Without them we wouldn't be complete human beings," it says in the Twelve and Twelve, the second major Alcoholics Anonymous publication. The book continues to say that the source of all of your problems is when your natural instincts get out of hand: "Our desires for sex, for material and emotional security, and for an important place in society often tyrannize us....Nearly every serious emotional problem can be seen as a case of misdirected instinct."

I'd like to focus on how we misuse one specific instinct — the preservation instinct. Psychology defines defensiveness as an unconscious effort to protect oneself, sometimes by distorting reality. We all use defense mechanisms. The trouble starts when we overuse them.

Defenses evolved for a reason. As animals, we had to defend our food and our family, and we had to defend against being eaten. Now that we generally aren't in danger of being eaten it makes no sense to walk around with defenses as thick as Humpty Dumpty's wall. The trick is to realize what you are defending against, bring your defenses into the light, explore them and toss out the ones you no longer need.

Most of the defense mechanisms you use to cope may have been useful at one time in your life, but are now weighing you down. You may be in denial or minimalize ("it's only weed"). You may rationalize (rather than "I'm a failure," you might tell yourself, "I never really wanted that career anyway"). Or, if you've had a lot of trauma, you may disassociate at times, feeling as if you have left your body, a common coping skill for a child who is helpless in the face of anything that might feel life-threatening. You may also attempt to flee from intimacy, fear or painful feelings by overeating, drug use, gambling, rage, sexual addiction or any other instinct gone awry.

There are three ways animals deal with threat: fight, flight or freeze. Some of us run from what we fear, and that goes for internal fears as well as external. Others just shut down like turtles or play dead. Another option is to respond in an aggressive manner to what feels like a threat.

Trauma specialists usually agree that you recover from trauma more quickly if you take action instead of freezing or fleeing. I had first-hand experience with this phenomenon a year ago, one night at 3:00 a.m., when I heard an intruder come up my stairs and then saw his shadow at my bedroom door. My knee-jerk reaction was to go straight toward the shadow and, in a voice I have never before heard and didn't know I had in me, I yelled, "What the f--- are you doing?" I must have sounded like the burglar's mother because he ran. I can't take credit for it, as I did not make a conscious decision to run a two-hundred-pound man with a screwdriver in his hand out of my house. It was simply instinct. And I was very, very lucky.

I am not sure if that is the safest way to act in a similar situation. At times it might be wiser to hide or run when there is a physical threat — you'll have to check with law enforcement for advice on that one. My point is simply that I did not suffer post-traumatic stress from the burglary and I believe that is because I didn't run and I didn't freeze — I took action. When I translate this into emotional health, I vow to stop freezing or running – to face my demons head-on.

When I taught creative writing in a prison facility for teenagers, all of them triple felons, I noticed that many of the kids wrote about experiences of physical and sexual abuse as young children, memories they had long repressed. When I asked the administration to tell me, just in general, what crimes led to their incarceration, I should not have been shocked to learn that the majority of these young boys whom I had grown so fond of were guilty of sexual offenses. I've often wondered what happened to those young men, but I bet that at least one life was saved by facing their demons in writing. I bet at least one of those kids saw what he wrote, remembered what he did — and put two and two together. Once you come out of denial and break though your defenses, it's hard to keep repeating the same destructive acts.

If your coping mechanisms are seriously compromising your well-being, I suggest that you seek professional help. You do not want to waste any more years being only half aware of what is going on inside. Trust me, I wasted my twenties spaced out, in denial and running as fast as I could. And I didn't do so well when the death of my sister coincided with my traumatic divorce. I didn't seek enough help and so I wasn't "all there" during years when my kids deserved an emotionally stable and fully present mother. So if you think it may be serious, it probably is, and I suggest you either find yourself a therapist or invest in a community of people to support you. There are many income-based clinics. I worked as a psychotherapy intern at the Maple Center in Beverly Hills and the lowest fee, as I recall, was fifteen dollars.

Bottom line is that you pay a huge price when you perpetuate unhealthy defense mechanisms. I believe the better option is to open up and let some light in. So instead of running from your feelings or living in the past, you learn to lead with your heart.

WARM UP

Write a little story in which you are a superhero with superhuman powers. Or you can just write what powers you would choose and why you chose those particular powers.

EXERCISES

A) Now look at any abuse or trauma you may have experienced in your life. No need to dwell on it right now, just name it in a few words. If there are many, make a list.

B) Write about how you dealt with these traumas. What coping mechanisms served you at the time? Are some of them outdated, no longer necessary? What price are you paying for holding on to these defenses?

C) If you did not cope well, how would you better navigate through those traumas knowing what you know now?

D) Writing in the third person (using she, he or a gender neutral pronoun), describe what you might be like if you let go of all those things you think are protecting you. Describe yourself with an objective and compassionate eye--your true, naked, vulnerable self. Would you be more present? Able to have better relationships? More inspiring to your friends?

Roots

My father was born on the same farm where his mother was born. In other words, the land was in my family for over a hundred years. I visited the farm every year until my grandparents died. I embraced their love and those roots with a deep respect for my elders along with the values that are my inheritance; and I believe this contributed to my resilience. I can't think of any other reason, aside from my grandmother's love and stability, that I survived all that self-abuse and tragedy and continue to thrive as I begin the third act of my life.

Your genes survived because your ancestors had both genetic strengths and the ability to learn skills that helped them navigate the challenges of life. So acknowledge those strengths and draw from them. Everyone in your life is influenced by what you put out there. So it is your duty to use those strengths to spread well-being and good will. And if there is negativity or especially mental illness in your family history, your job is to break the chain.

While I have the privilege of a strong family on my father's side, I also have the curse of another genetic line full of alcohol, suicide and various mental illnesses. For decades I resented my mother for undermining instead of being supportive of me, being jealous instead of celebrating my successes and wielding her power in abusive ways. Eventually, I came to realize that she had family curses she was not aware of and therefore could not work on. She never had an introspective life.

When I look at my mother's mother, who provided me with razor blades to cut my paper dolls when I was five years old and who also gleefully showed me the charred remains of a cat she had thrown in the incinerator, I realize that my mother did not create her "mean streak." She too was once an innocent child. She bore me when she was seventeen. She was the youngest of six, with four older brothers. I have no idea if there was neglect or abuse or if she was over-indulged. But it was easier for me to forgive her when I realized that anyone who lived her life might behave in some of the same ways.

I also began to look at the positive things about my mother, the useful traits she passed down, the fact that she is a very strong and incredibly successful woman. Taking inventory of the positive traits that I inherited gave me an opportunity to respect and embody the strengths in that side of my family.

Just as genes are passed down, so is our family's emotional history. Many studies have been done on children of Holocaust victims. Signs of post-traumatic stress disorder can be found not only in their behavior but in their actual blood chemistry. A study done with mice, separated from traumatized parents at birth, even showed a change in the genetic makeup of their offspring (and their sperm). A gene that was responsible for anxious behavior seemed to have been altered.

Just think about trying to raise happy children while you are suffering the aftermath of a horrific trauma. A parent who is anxious, depressed or traumatized is not likely to raise children who are cheerful, thriving and optimistic. The good news is that even in the most damaged of souls, there are almost always positive qualities and strengths that will lead you to survive and thrive.

Identifying both the baggage and the treasures that have been passed down gives you an opportunity to break the chain. One tool used by psychotherapists to explore the dynamics in families is the genogram. Kind of like a family tree, it goes further, allowing you to identify generational traits, relationships and patterns. Our exercises for this session will be to do a rough sketch of your genogram.

WARM UP

On a large piece of paper, create what looks like a
family tree (with your name in the middle). Leave
lots of room to write between the lines.

EXERCISES

A) Between each two people on the family tree, jot
down some words that describe their relationship.
Use words such as friendly, harmonious, doting,
idolizing, distant, caring, apathetic, controlling, hostile,
violent, abusive, estranged, etc. When you are done,
identify themes that may run through your genogram.

B) Write a paragraph or two about the individuals
that you know most intimately. What was your
relationship with your mother like? What was her
relationship with her mother like? Stretch a bit and
write down your hunches about a few other dyads
(pairs) in your family history.

C) In terms of any disturbing trends in your family,
declare in writing how you plan to "break the chain."
Give yourself credit for the work you have already
done.

D) Make a list of the strengths you have inherited.
Own them!

Growth

Surviving is important, but thriving is
elegant.
— Maya Angelou

One thing you can be sure of is that life is always changing, evolving, dissolving, moving. Nothing stays the same for long. As Heraclitus said, "There is nothing permanent except change."

When things get bad, we say, "this too shall pass," which means that it will get better or it will get worse, but it will for sure change. When life seems perfect, well, that too shall pass.

The cherry on the top seems to be that we will all get old if we're lucky. Funny how we look forward to our birthdays when we are sixteen or twenty-one, and then at some point, we start dreading them.

The beauty of aging is found in continuing to grow. Science says that if you continue to challenge your mind, it will continue to function well even in old age. It is only when you stop growing that the mind begins to lose its powers. Use it or lose it.

Growth, reaching for the sun, is the intention of life. Constantly striving to better one's self intellectually, spiritually, emotionally and morally is the job of a wise human. Your life is a work of art that only you can craft.

But growth takes time. As you are trying to break old habits and develop new strengths, the gentle path is to be patient with yourself. Ralph Waldo Emerson suggested we, "Adopt the pace of nature; her secret is patience."

Patience allows the feelings and then allows for them to pass. Impatience keeps you all wound up. The fears or obsessions you feel persist and fester as you hold on to that stance. Patience requires that you step back, take a breath. When you take the stance of patience, you enter the realm of the good parent, who is able to embrace the fearful child. Patience gives you distance from yourself — the detachment to observe rather than dwell on the feeling.

WARM UP

Write a "How to Age Well" list. You can be funny on this first round.

Here's mine!

HOW TO AGE IN HOLLYWOOD – A GUIDE FOR ACTRESSES

1.Try not to stand in a position where anyone will see you in profile.

2.Never go anyplace during the day. Remember that the entire social structure for women in Hollywood is based upon lighting.

3.Have at least one affair with a twenty-five-year-old so you know what an ass Michael Douglas really is.

4.Statistics from the Screen Actors Guild indicate that something like 40% of the income made by Guild members is made by females under 25, another 43% is made by men over forty. And 2% is earned by women over forty.

5.How do you think I feel? I was an actress until they retired me at 35.

6. It's as if you had no choice but to put on a cheaper and uglier dress day after day, week after week. How does one do this with dignity and grace?

EXERCISES

A) Now that you've written a humorous list, answer the last question in mine – How will you age with dignity and grace?

B) Describe who you would like to be in old age. Any role models?

C) Write a letter from your elderly self to yourself now. Include some well-earned advice!

Death And Grieving

> The more we have suffered in the past, the
> stronger a healer we can become.
> —THICH NHAT HANH, *TOUCHING PEACE*

Death can actually be a beautiful passage. I feel so honored and grateful that I was able to be present for my grandmother's passing. As sad as I was to see my beloved grandma drift into death, being with her at that time was one of the great gifts of my life.

In the last days before her death, she slowly and peacefully lost consciousness. Finally there was no indication that she could hear or see or move except that she was raising her elbow in a flapping motion. It looked as if she was trying to fly. My father mentioned a gospel song that he said was one of her favorites - "I'll Fly Away." I said I did not remember that song and my father, who never, ever sang, starting singing it. At that point, I recalled the melody and sang along with him. "Some bright morning when this life is over, I'll fly away…" My dad and I sang together for the first time ever at Grandma's bedside. She passed that night as my uncle read to her from the Psalms. She drifted off so peacefully that he did not even notice.

The sudden, shocking death of my thirty-four-year-old sister was an entirely different experience. My sister's death was infinitely more difficult and extremely challenging emotionally. When you have a shock to your system like that, a loss that shakes up your whole world, it is considered a trauma.

I am certain that it is partially because I did not have a substantial support network that it took me years to come to terms with Cami's death. Although I was in therapy, I had isolated within my marriage (big mistake) and did not have a solid community to carry me though.

There is a wonderful place in West Los Angeles called Our House that facilitates grief groups, and they can probably refer you to a similar facility in your community. Unfortunately, they didn't have sibling groups at that time, but simply meeting with people who were at the same stage of grief was of immense help to my mother, my sister's husband and my niece and nephew. The kids stayed involved with Our House for years, eventually becoming coleaders of groups with younger children who had lost a parent.

When someone dies an untimely death, I don't believe you ever "get over it." It just becomes a part of who you are. The good news is that the experience gives you the ability to really feel what others are going through and the opportunity to be of service.

Your own mortality also hits you in the face when a loved one dies. As far as we know, man is the only animal who is conscious of the inevitability of his or her death. Denial is the way some people deal with this. But it is wiser to come to terms with your own mortality. Knowing your life is finite makes each moment more precious. As of now, I feel at peace with the fact that I am going to die. There is something oddly comforting about liberation from the terror of the unknown. After all, matter doesn't disappear--it just turns into energy. I don't mind if the dirt I am in bears a flower that contains my soul.

My best buddy, René, used to work in an emergency room in Sweden and held the hand of many a dying person. He told me that there were two ways that people left this world. Some held tightly, squeezing his hand, fearfully grasping to life. Others held his hand gently and then simply let go.

I believe that your whole life is preparation to let go with grace. That takes a great deal of acceptance and generosity, all of which you must cultivate while you are still hanging around, so that you can let go gracefully when the time comes.

Steven Levine wrote a wonderful book called *A Year To Live*. He worked in hospice for many years and found that once people are diagnosed with a fatal illness, they usually do not have even a year left to live. The premise of his book is to live this very year as if it were your last.

There are many books on grief and dying so there is no need for me to attempt to do more than share these personal experiences and offer up a couple of exercises that I believe will aid you in the process of integrating the death of a loved one, as well as a couple of exercises that will help you look at your own mortality in a way that will enrich your life.

WARM UP

Write your own epitaph. Then write another one with a bit of humor thrown in.

EXERCISES

A) Write a letter to a loved one who has died. You can voice your anger if you have any, but also mention the wonderful experiences you had with your loved one and talk about what you miss.

B) Describe what you would do differently if you knew you only had one year to live. What are your priorities? What is unsaid or unfinished?

C) Write your bucket list – all the things you would love to do in this lifetime. Make plans to do one of those things.

WATER

"I have a feeling that my boat
has struck, down there in the depths,
against a great thing.
And nothing
happens! Nothing... Silence...Waves...
— Nothing happens? Or has everything
happened,
and are we standing now, quietly, in the new
life?"

—JUAN RAMÓN JIMÉNEZ

Water seems magical in its ability to change forms, coming to us as gentle rain or crystal snow, as crashing waves, flowing rivers, violent storms, calm lakes, and human tears. Like water, your life and emotions constantly change. You can exist in a cold and solid state, or you can flow with the current and ride the wild waves.

You may often long for, and sometimes feel, that primal place of total peace, like floating in warm water. Our lives began in an aqueous environment (to paraphrase psychologist Jonna Fries in this paragraph), in the safety of the womb, where we first started to have the experience of being. Not a care in the world, simply existing, floating, receiving. In some ways, usually unconscious, we seek to return to this all-encompassing warm environment even as adults. But seeking perfect comfort can lead to self-destruction as in addictive behaviors, messed-up relationships and excessive hedonism. Or it can lead to self-realization as in meditation, creativity, and positive relationships with self and others. Our default position is to return to the methods we adopted to get our needs met in early childhood. It is valuable to explore what these methods are. For example, in order to adapt, many of us created a false self. It is important to train yourself to recognize when you have abandoned your real self and to find within you a secure base, your own womb-like environment.

In one of the following exercises, I will suggest you either remember or create a place to go in your imagination where you are totally comfortable and relaxed, protected and at peace. I have a few. One is floating in the warm waters of the Caribbean just before the sun goes down. Other times I like to imagine myself in the palm of God's hand. Often, I just enjoy the memory of visiting Grandma's farm as a child, memories of fireflies, tire swings and gospel songs. These are the places that I return to whenever I am anxious or curled up in a fetal position because I just cannot deal with life at that particular moment.

You may or may not be able to remember a place where you felt warm and welcome. Students have written about their aunt's kitchen, the cubbyhole at home and a special place outdoors under a tree. Many of you probably never found a safe and comfortable place, but guess what? You get to create an ideal nest for yourself. Perhaps a velvet-lined womb-like cave or a fluffy cloud you can fall into and float. The sky's the limit!

WARM UP

Choose one word from each of the six rows:

bubble	floating	light
candle	treading	blue
wave	swimming	warm
surface	drowning	storm
dolphin	dreaming	deep
rain	crying	river

Use your chosen words and let these be a jumping-off point toward letting your pen flow. Allow each sentence to flow out of the previous one. It can be light or dark and it doesn't have to make sense!

EXERCISES

A) Imagine, on paper, your own perfect safe environment. Your safe place can be anywhere that you can imagine being perfectly comfortable and at peace. It does not have to be realistic at all – it can be a cave on the moon - any place that you dream up!

Once you have done this exercise, you will have created for yourself a place you can always go whenever you are stressed, depressed, fearful, or you simply want to relax. Practice going to that place in your mind so it will be vivid in your imagination and available when you need a retreat. Fighting at home? Take refuge in your safe place. Stressed? Take a five-minute vacation. Meditate on being held by the image you have remembered or created. A refreshing pause…

B) There is no better way to entertain a child than to put him or her near water. The ocean, the bath, the tiny plastic pool and the sprinklers. Children are naturally mindful. In other words, they are in the present moment.

Take some time to be mindful of your interaction with water. Feel the water on the palm of your hands as you wash them. Enjoy the splashing on your face as you do your morning ritual. Listen to the sound of running water. Take a bath and feel the bubbles dancing on your skin. Feel the non-resistance of the water, how it accepts and surrounds your hand, your body, caressing you as in the womb. Listen to the rain, and notice how clean everything is after a strong downfall. If you are near the ocean, watch the movement of the current. Notice the awesome power as waves hit the shore. When you have done this, write about the experience of mindfully spending time with water.

Going With The Flow

> "Acceptance receives the moment like water,
> yielding, absorbing."
> — STEPHEN LEVINE, *HEALING INTO DEATH AND LIFE*

When I first heard the phrase "just go with the flow," it was a hippie term, meaning be cool — whatever happens, happens. Why did I ruin my acting career by ending up on that beach in Mexico for two years then joining a circus and getting kidnapped in the process? In those days, I just went with the flow, which at the time meant going wherever and doing whatever felt best at the moment.

Going with the flow means something different to me now. Now I experience it as moving fluidly through life's ups and downs, becoming comfortable with the changes and transitions. Taking the action and letting go of the results. Relaxing and accepting what is. Riding life like a wave.

Going with the flow means letting go of the results. Take the action, do the work, keep the goal in mind, but you may as well relax about the results, because they are no more under your control than the course of a river.

Watch the way water flows, the path of least resistance. Feel the relief when you give up trying to control that which you cannot control. Feel how refreshing it is to let go of "I want it my way" and just say yes to the present moment.

The key word is "acceptance." Trying to control people, places or things is a futile battle. The *Big Book* of Alcoholics Anonymous talks about the importance of acceptance. "When I am disturbed, it is because I find some person, place, thing, or situation – some fact of my life – unacceptable to me, and I can find no serenity until I accept that person, place, thing, or situation as being exactly the way it is supposed to be at this moment."

Of course if a person is abusive or the place you're in is truly unacceptable, then run. But unless there is some reasonable action to take, fighting people, places and things is futile. It is just as impossible to change another person as it is to change the weather.

Now is all you have. You may as well accept yourself and your situation as it is in the moment. Forcing things to be the way you want them to be is like trying to open a door with a key that won't fit, no matter how many times you twist, push and jam it. If you find yourself gritting your teeth as you fight to make things look exactly like you would like them to, then stop trying to swim upstream!

WARM UP

Read the Juan Ramón Jiménez poem at the beginning of the chapter. Use a line from it as the inspiration for a poem, a paragraph or a page.

EXERCISES

A) Write about something that you are resisting, a situation that you are attempting to control or someone you are trying to change.

B) Contrast that with what your life would look like if you simply accepted that person or situation.

C) Write a poem or short-short story using acceptance as the theme and stating everything in the negative. It can be true, about something that is happening in your life or it can be fiction. (For example: Sam did not want to go. Molly did not like him anyway, so they never left their house. They didn't phone, they just didn't show up. But hey, I am not going to lose sleep over it!)

Thirst And Dangerous Waters - Addictions

> You f---ed with my heart
> You f---ed with my mind
> You f---ed with my soul
> You f---ed with my time
> — KRISTY LEE, *HEY CRAZY*

There is a reason why each of the other quotes in this book is inspirational and this one is full of assertive rage. It's a good one to sing at the object of your addiction, whether that be a person, a drug, food, sex, gambling or anything else that undermines your well-being or keeps you from thriving. Addictions are like bad relationships. They try to steal your time, your spirit and your belief in yourself.

Of course you are getting something out of it, but ask yourself if it is worth the price. And ask yourself what it would be like to live without that addiction. Who would you be?

I have been known to purposefully jump into dangerous water. Sometimes it was a drug that could have killed me, and a couple of times it was a relationship that could have killed me. I knew the warning signs, I knew the risks and dangers. I chose to ignore them — either for the sake of romantic ideation or immediate gratification.

They say you see all the warning signs in the very beginning of a bad relationship. A friend of mine, I'll call him Don, went out with a woman who was sneaking glances at Don's texts by their third or fourth date. A year into the relationship, she was so insecure that Don felt smothered. I said, "Didn't you see that coming?"

We all thirst for love, sex, food, shelter and spiritual connection. Some of our cravings are healthy and within reason and some are out of hand. The deciding factor is: Does it make you feel good about yourself or does it just leave you temporarily gratified?

Addiction is the ultimate result of our natural thirsts going awry. It is natural to want to feel comfortable, to want to forget our troubles, to want to loosen up or relax, to want to have sex. But to demand it immediately, without considering the consequences, is childish.

When you choose to satisfy your urges at the expense of your own health or welfare, or at another person's expense, you are in trouble. Your self-image is sullied and you don't feel good about yourself. And how you see yourself is what you are living off! I'm not saying that addiction is not a disease, or that it is easy to overcome. But the need for immediate gratification in an adult is inevitably destructive.

Ask yourself what the pain is that you are trying to kill. Usually it is trauma-based and often it causes you to isolate. That is the worst thing you can do for an addiction. Connection is what you need, what will heal you. So call that old friend. See them face-to-face and give them a hug. A few hugs a day will give you a happier life.

Healthy thirst brings to mind the biblical phrase "thirst after righteousness." The thirst to know truth and give love, the desire to live up to your values and the search for spiritual nourishment are all fulfilling quests. The need to have worldly goals and go after them in a way that doesn't harm others, to have attachments to other people, to create family and community — these are all thirsts worth quenching.

WARM UP

Take the quote at the beginning of this section and think of who or what addiction you might apply it to. Then write like hell – let them have it. And after you've filled the page then crumple it up and toss it!

EXERCISES

A) When have you ignored the warning flags and jumped into dangerous water?

B) Of course you're addicted to something! Make two lists: cost and benefits.

C) Write a list of the healthy things that you thirst for and what quenches those thirsts.

Thawing Ice, Raining Tears

> Sometimes it's bad when the going gets
> tough
> When we look in the mirror and we want to
> give up
> Sometimes we don't even think we'll try
> Sometimes we cry
> — VAN MORRISON, *SOMETIMES WE CRY*

I used to cry in yoga class. Still do sometimes. Coming home to my body, really inhabiting the home that I often take for granted or even deny, makes me aware of the tension or dis-ease that I am carrying. When I sit down to meditate, and allow and accept all the feelings that come up, I occasionally find a wall of cleansing tears to shed in order to get back to the joy of an open heart. When I allow my defenses to melt, I find myself relaxed in my body with full awareness of the moment and tears begin to flow. Nowadays, it is just a tear or two. But in the past, when I was in grief after my sister's death and a lot of my trauma hadn't been worked through yet, tears just streamed down my cheeks, seemingly endless.

Tears of grief, fear or loneliness are more persistent and destructive when they are repressed. The result is tense bodies, misplaced venting, and often, depression. When you dam your rivers, the waters get stagnant and foul creatures grow tails.

A light rain refreshes the garden. A well-needed rain is followed by a crisp clear sky. Once the tears fall from your eyes, you will see more clearly. In allowing yourself to cry, you have freed up space for more pleasant emotions.

The other thing I want to say about tearful emotions is not to run from them but recognize them and move toward them. Invite them in. Allowing your emotions will let them flow through you. Going toward fear will help you become fearless.

When you feel bad, you may get fearful that this is how you will always feel. Not so. Open your heart, allow the feelings and know that they will change. Once you become friendlier with those feelings you've denied, you will have more access to the natural beauty in sadness. Rejoice in your tears as they are a sign that you are very much alive!

WARM UP

Complete this sentence ten times: Just below the surface, I..."

EXERCISES

A) What did you learn about crying as a child?

B) How do you feel about crying now? Is it frightening or are you at peace with your tears?

How do you feel when others cry? Does it make you uncomfortable? Do you feel you need to fix it? Do you ever feel like it's your fault?

Find a photograph or painting that has a strong sense of rain or stormy weather. Describe what you see. Then put yourself in the scene and write a little story about what you are doing there and why.

Trust

> "When I judge sadness negatively and cut
> myself off from it, it becomes frozen, losing
> its tender quality that connects me to life."
> —JOHN WELWOOD, *BEFRIENDING EMOTION*

In order to allow yourself to cry or feel difficult emotions, you need to trust that you're not going to fall into some deep dark well. You need to trust that feelings are not going to kill you. And you need to be in an environment in which you feel safe.

Working with a therapist or in a group that feels cohesive can help you explore some things in your life that might be difficult. When it comes to groups, "cohesiveness" is the operative word. I notice a radical shift in my workshops if I have just one person who is not willing to allow him- or herself to be vulnerable or support others when they are opening their hearts. When the chemistry of the group is harmonious, people seem to go deeper and leave feeling warm and uplifted.

If you didn't have parents you trusted as a child, it might be difficult to form a community that will support you. A helpless child feels frightened when he or she doesn't have trustworthy caregivers. As an adult, it may then be difficult to trust others enough to allow yourself to be vulnerable. It becomes hard to discern who is and who isn't trustworthy. Two things to look for before trusting someone are if they consistently do what they say they are going to do, and if they support rather than undermine you.

It's important to have some boundaries when inviting other people into your life. When a friendship is beginning, try not to spill all the beans and bare your soul right off. Trust is earned as you take turns exchanging thoughts and feelings that become more and more intimate in a natural progression.

It is precious to develop friendships in which each of you can recognize when the other is flailing, and can reach out a hand, perhaps even suggest a new perspective or help gear you toward a different trajectory. Someone who can help pull you out of the undertow.

When I was seven, swimming for the first time in the Pacific Ocean, I got caught in an undertow and almost drowned. At least I thought I was drowning. Taken under by a wave, I was turned around and upside down, all the while thinking of how I never was going to get to grow up and have children. My future flashed before my eyes as if it was never going to happen.

The wave eventually spit me out. I looked for my parents, who were in their early twenties at the time. I found them on their towels, laughing with their friends, oblivious. It had been the most profound experience of my young life, and they hadn't even noticed.

Sometimes we do get sucked under. But now I make sure I have someone watching my back, that I have at least one person in my life who will know if I'm keeping my head above water. It's crucial to know that you have support, especially if you venture into the deep, either by choice, or because life throws you a hard ball.

When I had the series of losses I have spoken of, I was pretty much down for the count for a while. I realize in retrospect that I had isolated in my marriage and didn't have a big enough support system to help me withstand such an onslaught of pain. Eventually, I started reaching out to old friends and being honest about how bad I was feeling instead of trying to pretend everything was okay. I found that my most valuable friends didn't mind talking to me even though I wasn't cheerful. And the good energy that they shared lifted me up.

Once I had the support I needed, I was able to allow the grief process to take place, finally surrendering, sinking into the sadness. I eventually came to realize that loss simply has to be accepted as an inevitable part of life. I began to see a little light at the end of the tunnel and to know that I would get to the other side if I just trusted the process. I learned to have faith that no matter how powerful the waves of grief or panic are they will eventually pass.

Don't be afraid or ashamed to reach out when you are depressed or suffering loss. I have found that one of the best ways to get closer to someone is to ask for help. Most people welcome the opportunity to give support. As I've mentioned before, research has shown that the brain of the "giver" produces more dopamine (the "feel good" chemistry) than that of the "receiver."

Who you are is dependent on your social context – the people you hang out with and those you trust. When you were a young child, you had no choice about who to rely on. But as an adult, having friends around who will catch you when you fall is your responsibility. Building a community around you of trustworthy people gives you the safety net that makes bad times more bearable and helps you to trust the progression of life.

WARM UP

Write all the words you can think of that begin with
T. Next to that, list all the words you know that
rhyme with Trust. Pick three vital words from each
list and use them in a paragraph or two.

EXERCISES:

A) Finish this sentence: What I learned about trust
when I was a child was....

B) Who and what can you trust in your life now? Do
you hang out with people you don't trust?

C) Describe an ideal friendship.

D) List ways you can create a bigger support system
or nurture the support system you already have. Think
of old friends you can call, new groups you can join,
neglected friendships you can rekindle or repair. Then
take action – implement one of your new plans.

"What is this mind? Who is hearing these
sounds? Do not mistake any state for self-realization, but continue to ask yourself even
more intensely, 'What is it that hears?"
— Bassui

The funny thing about our mind is that it can observe itself. As I witness my own thoughts, I often find I am exhaustingly busy planning,
analyzing and thinking about the past and future.

Our minds are just too cluttered. We are all in over our heads
with the decisions modern life demands of us. Just going to the gro-
cery store can require a lot of thinking. When I was a kid, there were
only three cereal brands to choose from. Now there are dozens. The
more choices we have, the more we have to think.

I believe the mind is overrated. It is great for defining your values
and useful in planning your future and making decisions. It is good
for filing experiences away in its memory. But it can also tend to torture us with its chaotic thoughts, regrets, planning, blaming, judging
and an incessant need to make sense out of everything.

Freud believed that we tend to ruin our most gratifying experiences by thinking. It's a clunky process, thinking, and it often gets
in the way of that higher form of intelligence that comes to you
in the form of intuition, creativity and connecting with a universal
consciousness. Simply being still and focusing on your breathing is
so very restful, when you dare to stand naked without your thoughts.

When I was in graduate school for psychology, I studied the six
stages of moral reasoning as defined by Laurence Kohlberg. The
highest level in his model was that of a Supreme Court justice. My
final paper described what I feel is a seventh level of development
— which Kohlberg had speculated on — that of connecting with
mystical forms of experience, or a universal intelligence, as exempli-
fied in the life of Buddhist monk Thich Nhat Hanh, who, through
meditation, allows universal intelligence to act as his guiding prin-

ciple. You can see that I'm not a big fan of reasoning as the end-all
and be-all.

WARM UP

Just to play a few little tricks on your mind, first draw
a picture using your nondominant hand. Now see if
you can write a sentence with the same hand.

EXERCISES

A) Think of your heart as a character in a story, and
pretend it can speak. What does it want to tell you?

B) Write a dialogue between your mind and your
heart. Is your heart in agreement with your mind?
Who is the boss?

C) Journal in the third person. Tell about your day
using the pronouns "he" or "she" or "they." I suggest
continuing this challenge for a few days — writing
as if you were watching yourself think, feel, do.
Observing yourself is a form of mindfulness and
this exercise will help you to be more aware of your
thoughts, actions, and emotions throughout the day.

Change Your Mind —
Obsession And Negative Messages

Was there ever a decision you made or something stupid you said that rolled around in your head like a tape loop? Sometimes it feels like you can't escape your own mind. Intrusive thoughts torture you and often tell you lies. It can be so painful that you just want to yell, "Shut up!"

Obsession can be excruciating. If letting it go is easier said than done, try to simply listen to the haunting voices, as if someone else is talking in an obsolete recording. Or watch it from afar, allowing your higher self to bear witness to your less effective, less supportive, less constructive self.

There are many nasty tricks your mind may play on you, including bullying you with should or should haves, cravings like "I must get what I want" or insults like "If I don't do this right, I'm worthless." Some thoughts may get stuck in your mind from childhood and you don't even know that they are there – you simply act upon them.

For years, I was annoyed with my dad for nagging me when I left the refrigerator door open for two seconds. While I poured the milk, he would say "What's the matter with you!" (That was one voice I had to clear from my head!) He's eighty now, and my annoyance has remained for decades. Just recently, I called him on it, and he had a genuine moment of self-realization. "Mother always told me to close the refrigerator," he said. "I guess that's why I get nervous when it's left open."

Inner voices can plague you for decades, telling you things you don't need to hear. So watch out for mental messages that say there is something wrong with you. What if you changed those voices and changed what they tell you? Or interrupted the thoughts with a pleasant distraction? Or simply watched them come and go as you meditate? When you are plagued by the past or projecting into the future with a negative bias, why not rewrite the stories you tell yourself?

Here is an example of how I "reframe" a situation in my life: I don't want to move from the home that I've raised my family in, but it looks like I might. So I choose to see the opportunities in it. Perhaps I'll end up with friendlier neighbors. It will be cozier in a smaller house. Change is good. I'll clean out my closets. I don't want to hang on to the idea that I must have what I want. It just doesn't feel good. Why do that when I can get excited about a new adventure?

It is important to remember that thoughts are not facts. One of the premises of cognitive behavioral therapy is that if you change your thoughts, it will change how you feel. But negative thought patterns need to be recognized before they can be changed. So it is all about how you talk to yourself, if you must talk to yourself at all. I prefer to live spontaneously in the moment whenever I can. Living in the now even trumps changing your negative messages – you just bypass them!

When you look at the future, you might be up against some common examples of unconstructive thinking. *Catastrophizing* (one of my favorite words) is about believing that the worst-case scenario will happen. And when your self-esteem is shaky, you may be engaging in *selective listening* (hearing only the bad). Or when you are trying to figure out what's going on in a relationship, you may be *mind reading* — imagining what someone else is thinking. Any of these sound familiar?

WARM UP

Get the clutter out of your mind and onto the paper. Practicing this daily is good mental hygiene.

EXERCISES

A) Choose a specific age in your childhood in which you may not have had the guidance or encouragement you needed. Write a letter from your adult self to your child at that age, giving him or her all the support he/she needed. (There may be some grief in this process.) Know that whatever you did not get then, you can give yourself now.

B) Write a list of the negative messages you tell yourself. Then go over the list and restate each phrase with words a loved one or imaginary "perfect" parent might say. Or, if you believe in a higher power or some kind of personified energy, what would he or she say?

C) Carry a little notebook and every time someone says something positive to you, write it down. Also note whenever someone helps you (even in the smallest way) or when you help someone else. And describe times when you feel good about yourself, noting what you are doing right. Start this little notebook now by writing down the last positive feedback you either received or gave yourself. Learn to own it!

Journaling

Journaling often starts off as an intellectual activity, but soon, leaps of intuition and inspiration can be experienced. Writing about the events of your day, the sights and sounds, your observations and reflections, helps to ground you. Writing about dilemmas or decisions may bring clarity. You can give yourself a pep talk or bathe in a pleasant memory. You can even use your journal to practice future behavior. Your journal is like a friend or therapist who is always there for you and will always listen.

Use your journal to explore your past, and use it to dispel your trauma. But do not dwell on either. If you find yourself repeatedly writing about the same upsetting situation, you should probably be talking to a professional. Don't re-traumatize yourself by going over the minute details more than once. Once is a tremendous relief, more than that will likely bog you down.

After decades of journaling, I found I was getting bored with myself, because I repeatedly whined about the same things. That's when I had to get creative. I still cleared out the clutter every day, but I went beyond that. It was time to look toward a positive future and I used journaling as a vehicle to help me get there. I wrote about my future goals and dreams. I wrote about good things that happened during the day as a way of becoming more mindful. Journaling made me a better writer and eventually I started writing fiction. I don't feel good when I don't write at all, so I usually honor that with a regular writing practice. Creativity saves my butt!

During the course of this book I have scattered several journaling ideas you can use daily. Keep your eye out for them. One of them is journaling in the third person, as I have mentioned. You can also journal in the present tense instead of the past. Try journaling using only one-syllable words. Use dialogues when you are trying to make a decision or having an inner battle. Keep it interesting so you don't get bored with yourself. A daily gratitude list is essential and Savor the Moment (in the following exercise) will also make you more mindful of the treasures in your life.

WARM UP

SAVOR THE MOMENT: Find a moment in your day that brought you joy. It could be something tiny, like when you had a pleasant exchange with a clerk or you noticed something beautiful in nature. Expand on it, stretch it out, savor that moment. If you do this in your journal daily, you will become more attuned to the fact that even in the worst of days, there are pleasurable moments.

EXERCISES

A) One journaling technique I love is making lists. To-do lists, of course. But also a list of resentments, a list of goals, a list of your positive attributes, a list of pros and cons, a list of character traits or habits you would like to change, etc. So start by making a list of the lists you would like to write. Then choose one of those lists and make it. Keep your list of lists to refer to until you've made all the lists you planned.

B) Consider a situation during the week in which you feel you did not cope well. Rewrite the story, using better coping skills. This is good practice for the next time a similar situation arises.

C) Write about future dreams or goals as if they were really happening in the present tense. Enjoy your future successes!

The Good Life

Whenever I have a major decision to make, I journal about it. What are the pros and cons, what will life look like next year if I do or if I don't? And what does my heart really want? I also ask myself what would be consistent with the "Good Life" as I define it.

What makes a good life in your mind, and how do you get there? One way is by becoming clear about what your values are so you have a consciously selected compass.

Your values guide your life, whether you know it or not - moral values, like fairness or generosity, and non-moral values, such as knowledge and beauty. It is only by determining what your values are that you can determine whether the things you are pursuing are worth spending your life on.

I learned from Dr. Cheryl Armon in a class at Antioch University that the notion of the good life grows in stages, just like intellectual maturation or moral development. For a child, the good life might be having birthday parties every week. At another stage in life, it might be upward mobility and acquisition of things, prestige or security. As you mature, it may mean realizing your potential or getting satisfaction out of helping others.

Good work is valuable not only when the results are good but also when the process itself is uplifting. In our world, good work isn't always valued, but that doesn't mean you can't value it.

We are all in the pursuit of happiness. For some of us, that means peace of mind and the joy of spontaneity. To others, it is the ability to set goals and reach them, without dying of stress in the meantime. Most of us aspire to live in harmony with husbands or mothers or children and with our community. What does the good life mean to you?

WARM UP

Make a list of the ideals you most value. Rate them.

EXERCISES

A) Are there things you are doing that are inconsistent with your values?

B) Let us assume that your basic needs for food and shelter are met. Write about what the good life would look like to you. Is it consistent with your values?

C) Write a story (one page) about a character living your version of the bad life, and I mean an awful life of their own making. Cigarette butts on the floor, perhaps, dirty dishes stinking in the sink. Exaggerate and have fun with it.

Humor

Freud wrote a book called *Jokes and Their Relationship to the Unconscious*. He felt that laughter was a form of relaxing the rational mind and accessing the unconscious.

In one of my yoga classes, the instructor has us do "laughter therapy" for lack of a better term. Once one or two people get started laughing, the rest of the room eventually follows suit, as laughter is indeed contagious. We end up with a whole room full of people who can't stop giggling. Talk about getting those feel-good chemicals going!

Humor allows you to see a dilemma or situation from a more positive point of view. It can help relieve tension as well as help you recognize the preposterous places your mind takes us to. It's especially useful to be able to laugh at yourself!

There are all kinds of humor: plays on words, accentuating incongruity, jest. There are also destructive forms of humor. I used to be very sarcastic, and that is a type of humor that I am glad I grew out of. It preys on other people, using their defects against them. I broke my addiction to sarcasm when I read that the Latin meaning of the word is "to tear flesh."

WARM UP

Try writing a cartoon. You can use stick figures if you like.

EXERCISES

A) What are the forms of humor you enjoy? Do you ever use humor at another person's expense?

B) See if you can remember some of the funny things that happened to you and/or a favorite joke or comedy show.

C) How can you get more laughter into your life?

D) Write about a man smashing grapes with his bare feet when his wife comes out, naked and wet from her shower. What does she scream? What does he answer? Now write your own preposterous situation and see if you can make yourself laugh!

I have always marveled at the oddly separate categories called Body and Mind. Isn't the mind in the body?

On the other hand, we live in our bodies in a different way than we live in our minds. For our purposes in this chapter, let's define the word body as the physical structure you live in as well as the senses, which enable you to touch, see, hear, smell and taste.

Think about how often you take your body for granted. The beauty your eyes allow you to experience, the sounds, the smells, the ability to touch, with which you are so blessed. The legs that carry you around, the hands that feed you, and the arms that help you with so many tasks. How lucky are you? Even if you have physical challenges, you also have gifts. Yet we usually don't even think much about our bodies unless we are judging them or they are causing us pain.

Simply being aware of your body can bring you a sense of well-being. It is quite clear that stress is manifested in our bodies to the point that it can cause disease. But just checking in with your body often transforms uncomfortable physical sensations into a more relaxed home to live in. Just noticing what is going on with the body (that you so often ignore) causes a shift in how you feel physically.

Our bodies have a lot to tell us. In Zen Budhism, you find the idea of placing a question in your stomach and waiting for the answer to come from there. D.T. Suzuki describes the Zen term *kufu* as "not just thinking with the head but the state when the whole body is involved in and applied to the solving of a problem."

So start checking in with your body regularly, noticing sensations. Just noting what is going on is a mindfulness tool, keeping you present in the moment. It also allows you to make adjustments. As I wrote this, I noticed some pain or discomfort in my middle back and realized I was crouched over the computer. Sitting up straight now, my back is happier and for some reason, I am smiling!

WARM UP

Written Body Scan

(I'd like to first warn you that if you are a victim
of recent physical trauma of any kind, please skip
this exercise, as it may bring up feelings that would
be better dealt with in a contained therapeutic
environment.)

Read the following, remember what you can, then lie
down and practice it:

First, get in a comfortable position and check in
with your body as a whole. Feel the surface that is
supporting your body. Feel the air on your skin. What
is the temperature? Feel how your clothes contact
your body. See where you feel your breath – is it in
your chest, rising and falling, or the soft wisp of air as
it goes in and out of your nose? Or is it in your lower
belly?

Now, start with your toes and see what sensations
you feel. Perhaps a sense of tingling or numbness.
Feel where your toes touch each other. Imagine your
breath going down to your feet. When you are ready,
let go of that area and bring your attention to your
ankles, your calves, your thighs. Just check in. "How
are you doing today, legs?"

Continue to slowly move your awareness up your
body in this way. See if any part of your body has
something to tell you, and if so, write it down. Are
there memories associated with a certain area?
How about that powerful area of your pelvis? Open
yourself to whatever is already present.

Feel your chest expand and listen to your heart.
Perhaps you can envision the color, weight, density or
lightness of your heart. Maybe you can feel it beating.

The neck is an area where most of us hold tension. Or
perhaps you hold tension in your mouth, particularly
if you were raised with the phrase "Children should

be seen and not heard." You don't need to do anything about the tension. Just noticing it often allows it to start melting away.

Once you have done a complete scan of your body, see if anything has changed in the process. Write down anything physical or emotional that you may have noticed or experienced. Write about anything your body wants to tell you.

EXERCISES

A) Now simply describe your body, from top to bottom. Every freckle and mole, wrinkle and bone. What parts of your body do you feel good about? What parts need your love and respect?

B) Make a list of five things you can do to promote physical relaxation and comfort.

C) On paper, describe everything you see, hear, feel or smell in the room. The colors, the textures, sizes, shapes, smells, sounds inside and outside of your body, the taste in your mouth. This exercise is a grounding technique. If you ever find yourself spinning out, it will deliver you back to the present moment and bring you to your senses!

D) Write yourself a soothing bedtime story, with an atmosphere that makes you feel content and relaxed. You can use either your little story or a body scan to help you fall sleep at night.

Feelings

Emotions always have a physical component and that's what we call feelings. Anxiety might be described as a trembling in the chest or an overall creepy-crawly feeling. Sadness might be a pit in your stomach. Anger may make you squint your eyes. The cliché for worry is a furrowed brow.

Feelings are the bodily result of emotions. In the chapter Water, you looked at emotions and wrote about how they were dealt with in your family of origin. For now, you are going to use a set of feeling words and try to identify what you feel in your body or with your senses when you have certain emotions. Does a particular emotion cause flutters in your tummy or a knot in your throat? Does it make you feel warm or cold, heavy or light? Is there a shape to the feeling or a vibration? Do you feel tight or loose, tingling or numb?

One of the challenges in dealing with feelings is overidentifying with what you are feeling. Think about the phrase "I am anxious" versus the phrase "I have anxiety." It is so much more comfortable when you realize that you are not your feelings.

Another challenge is simply identifying them. You probably generally use a few feeling words, but there are dozens of more specific labels. The following exercises will help you name them, as well as identify the physical sensations that go with them.

EXERCISES

A) Complete the following sentences identifying how your feelings manifest themselves in your body or what you do with your body when you have that feeling. (I've listed a few examples to get you started.) You can also describe how you act or react to the feeling.

When I feel...

Angry, I...(do you clench your fists?)

Secure, I...(what is your posture like?)

Insecure, I...

Bored, I...

Anxious, I...

Happy, I...

Frightened, I ...

Confused, I...

Amused, I...

B) This next sentence completion exercise will help you to more precisely identify what you are feeling at any given time.

I feel...

Overwhelmed when...

Ashamed of...

Accepted when...

Excited by...

Disappointed when...

Satisfied when...

Defeated when...

Needy when...

Worried about...

Disgusted by...

Most alive when...

Capable of ...

Distraught when...

Courageous because...

Hopeful about...

Special because...

Peaceful when...

C) Create two characters. They can be realistic or fantasy (like animals or cartoon characters). Now take two of the feelings you've written about and give them to the characters. Next, have those two characters interact. Don't be surprised if your story is either funny or disturbing, depending on the feelings you chose.

Our Body's History

Our bodies contain much of our history. In fact, it has been said that memory, especially of traumatic events, is stored in the muscles. There is even a psychological therapy called EMDR or Eye Movement Desensitization and Reprocessing, which is used to unlock memories and recover from trauma.

Thankfully, there are also pleasant memories for each and every one of us. Here's an entry from my journal after a check-in with my body when I was tired and weary one day. Notice how just getting in touch with my body elicited memories:

"My face is tired and my eyelids are heavy, my eyebrows feel old and my face hangs a little. My eyes feel the most tense. And my stomach. But my legs feel relaxed, and I am enjoying the breeze from my fan on my skin. Until I was about seven, my grandmother let me play outside topless. I remember running around her huge grassy front yard. I recall kicking my legs in the air as they made my tire swing go higher and higher. What freedom and joy."

Then there are the physical traumas you have experienced, perhaps injuries or illness. Looking into the history of your body can bring up a lot. Is it one of strength and health, or have you suffered illness or pain? What was it like when you broke your arm? Are you living with any ailments now? Have you suffered any abuse or physical trauma?

A client who didn't want to be named was generous enough to share the following:

"I remember peeling the skin off the fingernail marks in my arms, from when my mother flew off the handle and hit me. I remember my face hot from being slapped and spankings that stung not only my bottom but my heart. It hurt me to my very soul and told me I was no good. I have learned that was a lie. I have learned to love and respect my body."

As this exercise illustrates, even in extreme situations, you can turn it around. You can come to a place where you respect your body, where you love it in spite of its flaws, in spite of the fact it isn't Photoshopped.

Our feelings about our bodies change within our life span. Were you teased as a child for some physical attribute? Did you feel attractive? Did you place a lot of emphasis on beauty, either other people's or your own?

Probably because I was molested as a child and again in my teens, I used to cover my breasts with my long hair. I didn't wear make-up or attempt to look sexy. I didn't realize back then that I was doing this because I didn't want men to look at me in a sexual way, but that's what it was about. Oddly enough, I only began to allow myself to feel attractive in my mid-fifties.

Which brings me to the subject of aging. Hey guess what? Everybody's doing it! How strange is it when you go to a high school reunion and all of your friends look different? Or when you see someone on the street that you think you know then you realize that person is twenty years old and that your friend would no longer look like that.

Those birthdays with a 0 on the end seem to be shocking at any age. Oh my God, I'm an adult now. Or whoa, I'd better have children before it is too late. Or how could this be, I'm middle-aged! It gets really strange when you are my age and have friends who are thirty and think about all the things that happened in your life before they were even born.

At every stage, there is a tendency to look back with regret or longing. Or look to the future with hope or fear. All the while missing what could be the best moments of your life.

WARM UP

Take a look at your changing perceptions of your body. What did you think of it in high school and how do you feel about it now?

EXERCISES

A) Write a brief history of your body and your feeling towards it. How have those feelings changed throughout your life span? Have you ever been too thin or too heavy? What kind of injuries or illness has your body experienced? Write about what you went through. Focus on your resilience, how you've compensated for physical defects or recovered from wounds.

B) How comfortable are you with your age? How do you feel about the fact that you are aging?

C) If this resonates with you, have a conversation (in writing of course) with one part of your body that is calling for attention. What is it trying to tell you?

D) Write a detailed letter of your appreciation for your body. Thank your body for all it does for you.

Sensuality And Sexuality

Sometimes confused with sexuality, sensuality is simply about the senses, particular the tactile sense. Of course touching someone's soft skin is sensuous, as is the smell of a sandalwood candle or a long bath if you are actually aware of the water on your skin.

You can create sensuous feelings with the lighting in your room or what you wear to sleep in. There is sensual music, sensual dancing. And then there are oysters and chocolate! Sensuality is all about enjoying seeing, hearing, smelling, tasting and touching. Being in the present with awareness is essential for enjoying your senses. We often get so swept up in whatever we are thinking about that we forget to notice what our senses are experiencing – the color of the curtains, the sound of birdsong, the feeling of a light breeze on your skin, the texture of velvet. A wonderful cliché is "Stop and smell the roses!"

We all need touch. Babies don't thrive without it – they often become despondent. Perhaps you've heard of Harry Harlow's famous experiment in which motherless monkeys were given a choice between a wire mother with milk and a cloth surrogate mother with no nourishment. The monkeys consistently clung to the cloth mothers, indicating that touch is vital for us semi-evolved primates.

For me, languishing kisses and reveling in the touch of skin is sublimely sensual, and often more pleasurable than the act of sex. And that brings us to the place where sensuality and sexuality meet.

I am not even going to touch the area of sexuality. I'm going to give you your exercise point-blank and let you do the writing about sex. What you will learn from this activity is much more expansive than anything I could say.

Are you ready? This is an optional exercise, but may intrigue you: Write your sexual autobiography. (See warning below before you begin.)

Now if you're like me, the idea is horrifying. In my case, the process entailed a lot of tears. My history starts out with a sleazy old producer sticking his tongue in my mouth when I was twelve. And it got a lot worse before it got better. I came of age in the late sixties when some powerful sick men got away with a lot more than would ever fly these days. And I was actually told more than once that it was selfish not to share my body.

Now, sexual harassment laws have been enacted and children are taught in school that their bodies are their own. We've come a long way, but young women still get harassed on the streets and date rape is way more common than we'd like to think. One out of six women in the United States have been victims of rape or attempted rape, and children are still sexually abused. Which brings me to a serious note about this exercise:

WARNING: If this does not feel safe – don't do it. If you have been physically abused or raped, particularly recently, I suggest doing this exercise with the supervision of a psychotherapist or not doing it at all. In many instances, writing about your past sex life can be the first step toward acknowledging and releasing old images that have been stored in your mind. But if you have been traumatized, you need someone to witness and contain the feelings that may be awakened. So make sure you have some solid support, someone with whom you feel safe.

WARM UP

Deep breathing: Breathe in to the count of four, hold four, breathe out four, hold four. Do a few rounds.

EXERCISES

A) Write the history of your sex life. Perhaps you can start off with the teenager in love, your first kiss. Or the time you lost your virginity. Or you may choose to focus only on when you were a consenting adult. And enjoy, in writing, the memories when sex felt right. Take note of how the meaning you give sex may have changed over time.

B) Now for something lighter! Let's drop sexuality and find a piece of art that is sensuous. Sculptures of the human body are and I am sure you can find photos of both sculptures and beautiful landscapes online. Using a piece of abstract art would also be interesting for this exercise.

When you have chosen your piece, write about it using all of your senses. Try and put yourself in the scene. Or be the sculpture and let it move. Taste the colors, smell the textures, touch the rain.

C) Next, make a list of sensuous pleasures. And indulge in a few this week, let's say at least one a day, starting today!

D) I also invite you to look for and savor those moments of sensuality with awareness of all of your senses. Find times when you are able to be really present in the environment. Practicing this will increase mindfulness and help keep you in the Here and Now.

SOUL

"There are two ways to live: you can live as
if nothing is a miracle; you can live as if
everything is a miracle."
-ALBERT EINSTEIN

I used to feel that I had a hole in my soul. All that I really needed was to accept and cherish that space so near my heart. I sometimes talk to myself as I imagine an ideal parent would, telling myself that I will take care of the little girl inside me, that I will always be there for her and that I love her for who she is. I know that I am responsible for filling my own emptiness.

My guess is that most of you have at least a tiny place of aching emptiness. If you listen, that longing will often tell you what you need. Usually what you need is spiritual -whatever you interpret that to be.

You can be an atheist and still use spiritual tools. You can even create an imaginary mentor to talk to if you don't like the idea of a higher power. Call it Personified Energy if you like. There is always something larger than you – look at the stars in the night sky. And if you really don't believe that there is a power greater than yourself go down to the shore and shout, "Stop!" at the waves.

Our predicament as humans, with all the mysteries and unanswered questions we must live with, can create a kind of existential terror. Practice making peace with that fear, relax into its commonality knowing it is a very human and real experience.

When I feel like I am willing to accept life on life's terms, I tremble a bit, knowing what that means. It is a commitment to being present for whatever life gives, including its lessons and losses. Tell life you are willing to live!

WARM UP

Define the word soul. Don't look it up as it's more important to know your concept of the word, what soul means to you specifically. Be creative and expansive in your description. If you have never thought about it before, good – be sure and write before you think!

EXERCISE

A) This one is perhaps the most important exercise in the book: Describe your ideal Wise Being — can be God, an Ideal Parent or a Personified Energy — anything you can envision respecting. It can be in the realm of art or nature or religion, it doesn't matter — just something that you know is more powerful than you.

B) Imagine, in writing, taking a walk with this Wise One. If you talk, what do you say? If you walk in silence, how does that silence feel?

Prayer And Meditation

"In the Sufi tradition it is taught that all
things in the universe are constantly in
prayer: every leaf and tree, every stone, the
snowfall on every mountain, and all the
night sky stars..."
— Peter Levitt, *Fingerpainting on the Moon*

I have no intellectual interest in debating the existence of God because I don't believe that she resides in the intellect. Prayer works in my life, even though I am unsure who or what I am praying to. I used to pray to the ocean and it served me well. "If it works, do it" is my philosophy.

An Atheist's Guide to Prayer: Think of something of great beauty, get down on your knees if you are willing and pray to that piece of nature or art. The ocean, a giant redwood, the moon. It may be just your sub-conscious you are silently speaking to – but please, just try it!

My grandmother got up every morning at dawn and prayed for hours. I have always felt she was the sweetest and strongest person I ever knew. And I've also always had a sneaking suspicion that when I was a teenager traveling the world, hitchhiking braless through Franco's Spain and taking hard drugs with strangers, it was Grandma's prayers that kept me alive.

I am not a particularly religious person. I love Jesus and respect the Buddha, but truth be known, I would probably be defined as agnostic. Yet when I need help to be the person I really want to be, silently speaking to something bigger than me helps me change. And when I need the strength to bear unbearable grief, praying helps me find that strength. When I am fearful or panicking, prayer helps calm me down, reminding me to take a deep breath, rest my ego for a moment and surrender my burdens. My heart opens to receive love and wisdom and to give calm and comfort.

Happy people are quite often those who use spiritual practices and embody soulful values. Don't believe me? Check it out. That person who always asks about you first, the one who makes you feel relaxed, the person who bears life's burdens gracefully. Find out what their practices are.

Prayer can be a long plea or an expression of gratitude or both. Or it can just be simple and short. Maya Angelou said that she has two prayers, "Forgive me" and "Thank you."

I have heard it said that prayer is speaking to God and meditation is listening.

Meditation is also about simply paying attention. Paying attention to your breath, to your footsteps, to the birdsong, to the heart of another. And it is about what I have most harped on – letting go of your thoughts (just watch them and say thank you) and going deeper than your rational mind.

In the beginning I could barely sit in meditation for longer than five minutes, and much of that time was spent thinking. Sometimes I would wander off into thought for several minutes before I even realized that I had forgotten to focus on my breath. My teacher told me that just concentrating for the length of one breath was enough. That I could do. And if you can become aware of the rising and falling of just one breath, soon you can add another and another until you find moments of stillness and a sense of calm.

When I allow myself the time to let go of planning and reflecting and busying myself, when I just listen to my breath, I sometimes become aware of feelings such as fear or loneliness, feelings I've been running from. It is in that awareness that healing takes place. Allow feelings of failing or shame or loss. Acknowledge, perhaps, the frightened child you've run from for years. Sit with anything that comes up and simply let it pass through you. By facing these feelings and breathing through the pain, you begin to be able to let go.

WARM UP

Write a little prayer or blessing for each person who is dear to you. Ask for what they might need and express gratitude for their existence.

EXERCISES

A) Set a timer and meditate on your breath for two minutes. Afterwards, if you were able to focus on even one breath, write about what you found in the space between thoughts. If you weren't able to at all, write about the chatter you heard until it's all out of your head. Then try two more minutes of silent breathing.

B) Consider the phrase "I am not I." What does it evoke?

Who remains calm and silent when you speak?

What remnants of you will remain when you die? (from a poem by Juan Ramón Jimenéz)

C) Write a prayer for yourself.

Power And Powerlessness

> The basis of the Buddha's psychological
> teaching is that our efforts to control what
> is inherently uncontrollable cannot yield the
> security, safety, and happiness we seek.
> — SHARON SALZBERG

I have to laugh (good-naturedly of course) at people who think that all the money and prestige they have amassed means that they are powerful. What an unfortunate misunderstanding. All that clout won't save you from the undertow. Nature wins out in the end.

True power is soulful. It is the strength to face whatever life brings you. It is striving to become a better person and the courage to live up to your ideals. It is the gift that when nurtured, inspires everyone around you.

It is vital to know what you have power over and what you don't. Be clear what is in your jurisdiction and what isn't. Differentiate between what you can control and what you can't.

You plant a seed and water it, but did you really create the cucumber? The seed is a gift, tending it is a discipline and a pleasure, but ultimately, you must surrender the results. You can't make the plant grow by pulling on it, or through stubborn will.

You are powerless over the aging of your body, but you do have some power over how healthy you are. You can exercise, refrain from smoking and drinking excessively, manage your stress, etc. But even that doesn't ensure that you will avoid some calamity.

In other words, you can take action, but you cannot control the results.

You can discipline yourself to do your best work but whether or not it is well received is not up to you. You can plan and dream and shoot for goals but you can't guarantee the outcome. You can even love someone deeply, but you can't ensure they will love you back, certainly not in the exact way you would like them to. You can do all the footwork in life, but you have to let go of the results.

Knowing what you can control, along with an awareness of what you can't, is extremely liberating. It will save you oodles of time and energy you might have spent obsessing or mind reading, manipulating or playing fortune-teller. You can also stop kicking yourself in the butt because something didn't work out. When you know what belongs to you and what doesn't you can let yourself off the hook and enjoy the powers you do have — your talents, gifts, and your ability to love.

My father always told me not to worry about things I can't do anything about. There is also no point in trying to change things that you are powerless over. Instead, turn them over to something bigger than you. As I've said, you have every right to create your own Personified Energy, specially designed to suit you.

WARM UP

Write the word "Powerless" in the center of a blank piece of paper. Draw lines radiating from the word and place a word that comes to mind at the end of each line. Say one of the words that relate to powerless might be "aging." Like a family tree, draw lines outward from each word that related to powerless. Then draw lines from the secondary word. Now what does aging bring to mind? My first two thoughts are wrinkles and Buddha (because he talked about sickness, suffering, old age and death). So you write those words down. Keep doing this until you fill the page.

EXERCISES

A) List all the things that you are powerless over.

B) Write a letter to your Wise Being asking it to take your burdens – to take care of those things you are powerless over.

C) Spell out the word "Powerless" vertically, one letter at a time, on the left side of your paper. Now write a poem in which each line begins with a letter in the word P-o-w-e-r-l-e-s-s. (If the word "poem" is too intimidating, just write phrases.)

Forgiving

> "Always forgive your enemies; nothing
> annoys them so much."
> — OSCAR WILDE

Raymond Carver wrote an amazing short story about a family who had ordered a birthday cake for their child. The baker was furious when they didn't pick up the personalized cake. He left several phone messages, each one angrier than the last. As he nursed his rage, he had no idea that the child had been hit by a car and killed that week.

Even if it is a huge justifiable rage, as when your spouse betrays you, a parent abuses you or someone harms you physically, holding on to it only hurts you. The Buddhists say that holding on to anger is like grasping a hot coal with the intent of throwing it at someone else — you are the one who gets burned.

I am so impressed by the people who go to prison to confront and forgive the man who murdered their child, a seemingly unforgivable horrific man-made tragedy. As generous an act as that is (I doubt I would be able to do it) the victims also forgive for the good of their own hearts. I believe that the act of forgiving brings a touch of peace to even the most unspeakable pain.

On a lighter note, there may be people who simply continue to insult, undermine or abuse you, perhaps a boss or sibling or parent. Forgiving them does not mean you have to keep putting up with the same old thing. You only have so many cheeks to turn. Fool me once, shame on you; fool me twice, shame on me. If the object of your resentment continues to do the same thing over and over, do the work to forgive them, but also get out of harm's way.

One tool that aids in forgiving someone (in the moment) is to give that person something, even if it is just making them a cup of coffee or getting them a soda. I have tried this and it definitely helps diffuse my anger. Another tool for ridding yourself of resentments is prayer, even if you are an atheist. Whether you pray to God, to the birds in the sky or even to your own subconscious, ask for that person, the one whose actions you loathe, to have everything that you would ever want for yourself. Pray for them consistently over a period of weeks. This is a bit of A.A. wisdom that has kept many a furious person sober.

The one person you need to forgive the most is yourself and trust me — I am going to listen to every word I write, as I have not fully accomplished this monumental task myself. Most of my regrets stem from the periods of time when I was drinking and using excessively, the wasted years, the trashed career, the frivolously spent money and the reckless way I treated my body. My most painful source of remorse and self-flagellation are the memories (or lack of them) of times when I was not fully present for my sister or my kids.

But there is simply nothing I can do about the past. By not forgiving myself, I just perpetuate the pain I have already inflicted on myself. There is a statute of limitations on most crimes and only the worst criminals are imprisoned for life. Why should you be?

When you have been treated poorly as a child, it is easy to continue to abuse yourself, especially if you have in fact behaved badly. Perhaps forgiving yourself means calling on the nurturing parent inside of you, the one who would never beat or berate you, much less continue to do it for years. Perhaps you may not know that parent yet. That is something to focus your energy on – every time you start to suffer remorse, imagine a caring parent or Wise Being forgiving you. Feel the love!

WARM UP

A Gift from Nature

Think of someone you resent. If there is no one, think again. Pretend you can give a gift to this person. It can be anything from nature, a flower, a bolt of lightning, a ray of sunshine, a river…Write what you would give them and why. Tell what it feels like to give.

If you didn't get to forgiveness during this exercise, don't feel bad. Here's an example from a friend who tried the exercise:

"I'd love to give my mother a rose and rub the silky petals onto her cheek when she is sick and vulnerable. My mother's skin is soft and sometimes I want to tear it off of her. Tear — tear why are they spelled alike?"

EXERCISES

A) Write a letter to yourself, using the second person (referring to yourself as "you"), forgiving yourself for each burden you still carry.

B) Write a dialogue — a fight between two talking animals. Just for fun, write the whole thing using one-syllable words.

C) Do "A Gift from Nature" again. Only this time — the gift is for YOU!

Thank You

> "Got no checkbooks, got no banks. Still I'd
> like to express my thanks — I've got the sun
> in the mornin' and the moon at night."
> — IRVING BERLIN

No matter how bad your life is at any given point, even in the worst of times, there are always things to be grateful for. There are nice moments in each day. Gratitude balances the "I wants" by acknowledging the "We haves." A practice of appreciating the good things in your life nurtures feelings of optimism and joy. It also gets your ego out of the way so your spirit can shine.

A minute of gratitude is like a vacation for your heart and mind. You cannot be busy worrying about the future and bemoaning the past while you are consciously grateful for all the precious little gifts in your life. And just as the runner gets a second wind and is stronger with every run, gratitude is strengthened by repeated effort.

I am grateful for nature as I smell a sweet rose, am awestruck by a giant tree, and marvel at the colors of the sunset. I am grateful for whatever is healthy about my body. I am grateful for the friends in my life who help me and I am thankful for the opportunity to help them. I am grateful that I have shelter and plenty to eat. I am grateful for the wool socks that are keeping my feet warm. I am grateful to be able to laugh, especially at myself!

As I express my gratitude, warmth fills my body, a little smile perks up my face and I feel a bit more peaceful.

Gratitude will give you joy, hope, even faith. The more you practice gratitude, the stronger you will be to withstand difficult times, for there is always something to be grateful for, no matter what your circumstances are at any given time.

WARM UP

List the gifts you carry, the gifts you were born with or have been blessed with.

EXERCISES

A) If you haven't already integrated the exercise "Savor the Moment" in your daily journaling – do it again now. Choose a moment that was pleasant, a small moment you are grateful for and savor it in writing.

B) Write a thank-you note to someone to whom you feel grateful.

C) Write a gratitude list. What all are you grateful for today? If you do this daily, I promise your life will change!

Congratulations!

Writing is not easy and some of these prompts are quite challenging. However many exercises you did or didn't do and whatever the results – you did a good job just by sitting down with pen and paper. If you used a computer, you will have to start all over from the beginning. (Just kidding, but most of the exercises *are* repeatable – you will get a different result every time.)

I am honored that you spent the time to work and play with me. I hope the experience was, at various times, helpful, surprising, difficult and fun, and most of all, that it has inspired you to continue to write!

References

Bly, R. (2015) News From The Universe. *Counterpoint Press*. 96.

Byrne, N., Schutte, J., & Wing, B. (2006). The effect of positive writing on emotional intelligence and life satisfaction. *University of New England*. 62, 1291–1302.

Burton, C. M., & King, L. A. (2004). The health benefits of writing about intensely positive experiences. *Journal of Research in Personality*, 38, 150–163.

Cameron, L., & Nicholls, G. (1998). Expression of stressful experiences through writing: Effects of a self-regulation manipulation for pessimists and optimists. *Health Psychology*, 17, 84–92.

Cooper, D., Golden, L., Hall, L., Haggerty, J., Malouff, J., Schutte, N., et al. (1998). Development and validation of a measure of emotional intelligence. *Personality and Individual Differences*, 25, 167–177.

Diener, E., Emmons, R. A., Larsen, R. J., & Griffin, G. (1985). The Satisfaction With Life Scale. *Journal of Personality Assessment*, 49, 71–75.

Jimenez, J. R. (2009). *The Poet and the Sea*. New York, NY: White Pine Press.

Juline, Kathy. "The Intensive Journal Process: A Path To Discovery, An Interview With Ira Progoff". *Science of Mind Magazine* 1992

King, L. (2001). The health benefits of writing about life goals. Personality and Social. *Psychology Bulletin*, 27, 798–807.

Pennebaker, J. W., & Beall, S. (1986). Confronting a traumatic event: Toward an understanding of inhibition and disease. *Journal of Abnormal Psychology*, 95, 274–281.

Smyth, J. M. (1998). Written emotional expression: Effect sizes, outcome types, and moderating variables. *Journal of Consulting and Clinical Psychology*, 66, 174–184.

CPSIA information can be obtained
at www.ICGtesting.com
Printed in the USA
FSHW02n0156240818
51618FS